HEROES OF AMERICAN JEWISH HISTORY

Revised Edition

by

DEBORAH KARP

edited by

Benjamin Efron

picture editor
Sol Scharfstein

KTAV PUBLISHING HOUSE, INC.
New York, New York 10002

Liza

ACKNOWLEDGEMENTS

The Publisher expresses gratitude to Mr. Bernard Wax, Director and Dr. Nathan M. Kaganoff, Librarian, for the privilege of utilizing the research facilities of the American Jewish Historical Society. We also wish to thank Miss Susan Landy for her generous and knowledgeable help in suggesting and locating the photographs in the Archives of the American Jewish Historical Society.

PHOTOGRAPH CREDITS

AFL-CIO, 116; Alliance Israelite Universelle, 111; Amalgamated Clothing Workers Union, 117; American Jewish Archives, 96, 97, 98, 148; American Jewish Committee, 142; American Jewish Historical Society, 18, 19, 23, 26, 27, 31, 32, 33, 34, 36, 37, 38, 39, 40, 42, 44, 45, 46, 47, 48, 49, 50, 51, 54, 56, 57, 59, 60, 61, 62, 63, 64, 65, 66, 67, 68, 69, 70, 71, 74, 75, 77, 78, 79, 80, 81, 82, 83, 88, 90, 91, 92, 93, 94, 95, 97, 100, 104, 106, 112, 113, 114, 115, 117, 118, 119, 121, 122, 124, 126, 129, 141, 143; B'nai Brith Archives, 84; Dropsie University, 86; Educational Alliance, 122; Temple Emanuel, New York, 97; Hadassah, 108, 135; Harper's Weekly, 3; Harvard University, 43; HIAS, 130; Jewish Defense League, 150; Jewish Historical Society of England, 73; Jewish Theological Seminary of America, 99, 135, 148; Henry Kaufman YMHA, 124; Library of Congress, 5, 52, 142; Massachusetts Historical Society, 50; Metropolitan Museum of Art, 8; Michigan Historical Society, 93; Mount Sinai Hospital, New York, 60; Museum of the City of New York, 4, 114, 115, 122, 123; National Park Service, 28, 102; New York Federation of Jewish Philanthropies, 150; New York Public Library, 50; New York Times, 126; Pennsylvania Historical Society, 53; Radio Corporation of America, 126; Rhode Island Historical Society, 55; Student Struggle for Soviet Jewry, 149; Touro Synagogue, 31; United Jewish Appeal, 131; United States Military Academy, 67; Henry Francis du Pont Winterhur Museum, 41; Yeshiva University, 121, 148; YIVO, 110, 111, 120, 144; Zionist Archives, 125, 126, 130, 133, 134, 136, 141, 145;

Every effort has been made to identify and credit the source of each photograph, illustration, map, chart, translation, etc., in this book. All corrections or supplementary data in the identification will be appreciated and acknowledged in subsequent editions.

SBN 87068-394-2

NBP-90

MANUFACTURED IN THE UNITED STATES OF AMERICA
LIBRARY OF CONGRESS CATALOG CARD NUMBER: 72-5027

Liza

TABLE OF CONTENTS

A Note to the Reader

When you hear the word "hero," what do you think of? In my dictionary a hero is defined as a person of great courage, who is admired for his brave deeds and noble qualities. If this is your idea of a hero, then you may wonder why the Jewish men and women, about whom you are going to read, are called heroes. For they were not spectacular persons. Most of them were simple human beings who came to America to make a new life, men and women who wanted a chance to work and live in a land of freedom.

Yet, even though they were mostly plain people, they were in their own way, "heroic." They were not afraid to struggle and work hard. They accepted the challenges of pioneer life in America, of loneliness, of danger from attacks, of floods and sometimes even hunger. They were willing to stand up for their rights. The Jews who came as immigrants, and those who were born here, had strong characters and backbone. Many were courageous in battle. They took part in all the struggles for independence, for civil rights, workers' rights—in short, together with their Jewish and non-Jewish neighbors they helped to make this a great and democratic country.

In this book about the Jews in America you will find a number of Hebrew and Yiddish words. They are written in English, spelled out to sound like the word in the original language, and are explained in the story itself. But some of these words need more explanation, and since this would interrupt the story if the author stopped to explain them right then and there, we have placed an asterisk (*) after those words. This means that they are more fully explained in the dictionary in the back of the book.

Some English words, too, have an asterisk after them. These are also explained in the special dictionary in the back.

This book tells its story in pictures, as well as in words. We suggest that you look carefully at the pictures and charts and maps, for they are more than pretty and interesting illustrations. They are actually part of the story we are trying to tell, the story of a people who built a new life in this country together with the other newcomers to this land. At the same time, however, they held fast to the Jewish values and traditions they had brought with them from the Old World.

We think after you have read this book you may agree with us that these people can be called heroes. And we hope that you will have enjoyed reading about them.

Benjamin Efron,
Editor

Introduction

An Interview With You

Have you ever been interviewed?

What if a TV reporter were interviewing you? The first thing he might want to know is, "What is your name?" and then, "How old are you?"

He might ask what school you go to, and what grade you are in. "Do you like school?" he may ask. "Are you a pretty good student?" We hope you will be able to answer "Yes."

If the interviewer asks where you come from, you will tell him where you live. He may ask if you have always lived there. You may tell him that you were born there or that you come from a different city. If he wants to know more about you, he will ask about your family. He will find out what your parents do and where they come from. You will probably tell him that you and your parents and grandparents are all Americans.

Let us suppose the interviewer really wants to know all about your family. He may ask what country your ancestors came from. Would you know what to tell him? Do you know where the grandparents of your grandparents were born?

If you look back far enough, you will be sure to find that your forefathers came from another country. That is, unless you are an American Indian!

Every family in the United States and Canada, except for the Indians, comes from ancestors who were immigrants. These ancestors came from Europe, or Africa, or perhaps Asia, sometime in the last few hundred years.

Millions of immigrants came from Europe to America in the years before World War I. This is a scene at Ellis Island in New York Harbor, where most of the newcomers were received.

1

A drawing of early New Amsterdam, which later became the city of New York. Jews were among the early settlers in the Dutch colony.

The First Settlers

You know that Columbus was the first explorer to open the Western world to the people of Europe. Other men who explored North and South America came from Spain, Italy, Portugal, France, England and Holland. People from all these countries came to settle in the areas which Columbus and the others discovered. A few years after the white settlers came, the blacks first set foot in the Western world when they were brought in as slaves from Africa.

The first English colony was established in North America, in Jamestown, Virginia, in 1607. The Pilgrims came to Massachusetts in 1620. The first group of Jews arrived thirty years later, in 1654. They came to the colony that was called New Amsterdam, which had been started by the Dutch.

These first Jewish settlers had come from Recife, Brazil. In the years when Recife was ruled by the Dutch, Jews could live there freely. However, when Portugal

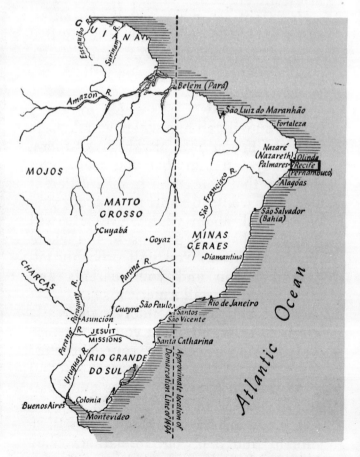

Map of the early settlements in Brazil. Recife is on the coast. It can be seen that this good harbor would be desired by the surrounding Portuguese colonists.

conquered the area, there was freedom only for Catholics. The Jews had to leave. Some of them came to New Amsterdam because there they hoped to be able to keep their religion. Like the Pilgrims and other immigrants who settled in America all through the years, they came here seeking freedom and a better life.

In most of the old world, people were not free to live as they wanted. European countries had been settled a long time. Some people owned very large farms and many had no land at all. Often there was not enough work or food. Most people worked very hard all their lives, but remained poor. There were many places where only one religion was allowed, and people of different religions or beliefs were persecuted* and sometimes put to death. In many lands there were men and women who felt that if they stayed, life would be hard for them and their children, and there would be little hope or promise for the future.

Many such people came to America. There was much more open space here, where a man could make a clearing and start a farm of his own, instead of being a farmer on the land of a king or nobleman. Workers and traders were needed to blaze trails and to build up cities. Each person was needed for the work he could do.

The building of railroads made it possible for the United States to expand westward. Railroad workers, shown here in their covered-wagon settlement, often remained in the areas they had helped to open for others.

People of many different types met and grew to know each other.

Of course, not everything was perfect here. There were problems and prejudices* in the new country too. Many of the immigrants brought with them some of the unfriendly feelings toward people who were different which they had learned in their birthplaces.

Here in America, however, settlers in the early days did not have to feel that they were strangers among a people who had been living in the land a long time. All were newcomers together. The feeling grew that anyone who wanted freedom for himself had to allow freedom for others. America became one of the first countries in the world to give religious liberty to all. It was a great thing that people with different beliefs and ways of life could still live and work together.

Back To The Interview

Through the years, millions of hopeful immigrants came to the American continent, looking for freedom and opportunity. You can ask your grandparents when the first members of your family came. Was it two hundred years ago? One hundred? Fifty? When?

Maybe they can even tell you something about the old country and the way your ancestors lived there. They may be able to tell you exciting stories of how your forefathers came to America. They may remember what it was like for your family when they first arrived here.

Like all immigrants, your relatives probably had some problems at first. They had left their families and had come to a land where they had to learn a new language and new ways of work. For

Castle Garden, a famous building at the tip of Manhattan that became the first reception center for new immigrants to the United States, in 1855.

4

them it was a strange land, but they had faith that their children would feel at home here. They worked hard so that their children could go to school, study, and learn to become good citizens. They knew above all that there were no special laws against Jews in this country, and that they would be able to hold to their religion freely and proudly.

If these first members of your family who came to this country could see you today, they, like the interviewer, might want to ask you some questions. They might ask if you are glad that they came here, and made it possible for you to grow up in this country. Would you thank them for being able to live in a free land? Are there other reasons why you feel grateful?

They might ask if you make good use of the freedom which America offers its people. They would be happy to hear that you are able to live as a Jew and to go to a religious school. Your pride in being a Jew would please them greatly.

They would also be glad to hear that Jews take part in all activities of American life. They would be interested to know about Jews who work for freedom and brotherhood, and about those who do good deeds and help others. They might also ask you what you are doing to keep and extend the freedom they passed on to you.

Would you be able to give a good answer?

This prayer room for Congress, the first in congressional history, was opened in 1955. The window's main panel shows George Washington praying for all America. Behind him, a verse from *Psalm 16*. The room is used by all faiths.

CHAPTER I

First In The New World

Who could be sure the world was round? Wise men said so, but most people could not believe it. They said, "Anyone can see with his own eyes that the world is flat."

Traders from Europe had always traveled east on land and sea to get to the isles of the Indies, and a long difficult journey it was. They could not understand how it would be possible to reach India, China and Japan by going the opposite way across unknown seas.

Christopher Columbus And The Western Route

Christopher Columbus was sure it could be done. For years he begged the kings of Europe to help him with his plan, to give him ships and men. He kept telling the rulers that the first nation to find an easy, all-water route to the Orient would be able to bring back many more shiploads of tea and spices, gold and silver than they could by taking the long journey eastward. The cheaper and faster way to these treasures, he insisted, was by traveling west.

"Spain will gain wealth and glory," Columbus told the Spanish Queen Isabella. The queen listened, but she and King Ferdinand knew that the royal treasury was empty as a result of their war to end the rule of the Muslim Arabs in Granada.

"We have no money to spare for such a dangerous voyage," the queen said.

Columbus left the court. Sad and weary, he mounted his horse and rode away. He was hardly six miles from the

Christopher Columbus, a portrait now in the Metropolitan Museum of Art.

city when a messenger on horseback rode up behind him.

"Come back sir, come back! Her majesty, the Queen, wishes to see you again!"

Full of hope, Columbus returned to the court. Four men were there, waiting for him.

"I am Luis de Santangel. I am the private treasurer to King Ferdinand," said one. "As soon as you left, I was bold enough to speak to the Queen. I told Her Majesty that I am willing to give my own money to help you carry out your plan."

"The Queen sent for me," said the second man. "I am Gabriel Sanchez. I am the treasurer of the whole land. I know how little there is in the royal treasury. That is the reason I am in favor of your voyage. This is the great chance to make Spain rich once more."

The two other men were Abraham Senior and Isaac Abravanel, who were advisers to the king and queen. They wore velvet skullcaps that showed they were Jews. The first speakers were *conversos,** Jews who had become Christians.

"Our gracious queen has asked our advice," said Abraham Senior. "Now that she and the king have cleared the country of the Moors, we look forward to a time of growth and new trade for our land."

There were Jews living in Spanish provinces from the time Rome ruled that part of the world. When Muslim Arabs conquered and ruled parts of Spain in the 7th and 8th century, more Jews entered the country and lived there in peace most of the time. They worked as merchants and traders, scholars, doctors, astronomers and poets. Some were statesmen and advisers to kings. It was such a good period for Jews that we speak of it as the Golden Age of Spanish Jewry.

Isaac Abravanel, the most respected of all the advisers, spoke last. "Many of my friends would be interested in helping you to reach new lands and find new ways to travel to faraway places. Spain would have new places for trade. We will help you."

Isaac Abravanel, adviser to kings in Portugal, in Spain, and later in Italian cities, was a loyal Jew and a scholar who wrote about the Bible and Jewish philosophy.

The queen had confidence in her advisers and in their promises to help. The king and queen signed a paper which made Columbus an Admiral. They gave him the power to outfit three ships that were to sail across the Ocean Sea to find a new route to the Indies.

The Ninth of Av

At about this time the queen was busy with another matter. Tomas de Torquemada, her religious adviser, had come to see her one day.

"Your Majesty," he said, "by the help of God you have cleansed Spain of the

7

Moors. But that is not enough. For all the people of your land do not yet have one religion; Spain is not yet truly Christian. Many Jews have become members of the Church. That is good. But there are still far too many, hundreds of thousands of them, who are not convinced. Not only are these Jews stubborn in holding onto their faith; they are also a bad influence on their former brothers who have joined the Church."

The queen listened carefully to what Torquemada said.

"Again and again we see that they try to lead the conversos astray," Torquemada continued. "They give them prayer books and Hebrew Bibles. They deliver meat prepared in Jewish fashion to their back doors. On Passover they smuggle *matzot** to them. They welcome baptized Jews secretly to their prayer meetings. The Church cannot relax its watchfulness until there is not a single Jew left in your kingdom. It is God's wish,

Tomas de Torquemada, fanatical leader of the Inquisition, which persecuted untold numbers of Jews and Christians in the name of the Catholic Church.

and the Inquisition* will help to make Spain a totally Christian land."

This was what Queen Isabella also wished with all her heart. She wanted above all to keep the Church strong. "The synagogues can be turned into churches," she said to herself. "The wealth of the Jews will be turned to a good purpose. Some will go to the state and some to the Church."

She discussed this with King Ferdinand. "So long as Jews live in our midst the New Christians are tempted to return to their old ways. Many have been brought to the holy court of the Inquisition and their sins have been discovered."

Isabella and Ferdinand agreed. "We have been able to unite Spain and drive out the Moors with the help of the Church. It is a sign that we must use our

When the Christian kings and nobles defeated the Muslims and came to power in the Spanish provinces, hundreds of thousands of the Jews who had been living a long time in the country stayed on. It was their home and they expected to carry on their lives as before.

Some fanatic Christians, however, wanted to convert all the Jews. Monks of the Dominican Order, especially, stirred up the people against the Jews. A very bad attack took place in 1391, and there were several more in the next century in Seville, Toledo, Barcelona and other cities. Thousands were killed without mercy.

In these troubled times, churchmen offered Jews the choice of "the sword or the cross." Many Jews allowed themselves to be baptized in order to save their lives. In this way a large number of conversos or New Christians grew up in Spain.

In Spain and Portugal, and in the colonies of the New World, church members spied on the New Christians for signs that they were not true believers. The fact that no smoke came out of their chimneys on the Jewish Sabbath, or that they had a festive family dinner at Passover time, or a clean white tablecloth was used Friday night, would be enough to cast suspicion on them. The spies would report them to agents of the Inquisition, who would arrest them for questioning.

Suspected Marranos were brought to trial as "Judaizers." They were not allowed to have lawyers for their defense, nor see their accusers. They were often tortured to make them confess. If the Inquisition declared somebody guilty, he was condemned and handed over to the king's soldiers for punishment. This took place at a ceremony called an "auto da fe." Thousands of such men and women were tied to stakes and burned to death in public view, as an example of how people would be treated if they were false to the Church.

Burning at the stake of a victim of the Inquisition. Thousands were brought to trial and condemned in many countries, during more than three centuries of the Inquisition.

power for the good of the Church."

A new order went out. It said that all Jews must leave Spain in four months' time. A wave of shock and despair swept over the Jews of Spain.

True, it had been getting harder for them to live in Spain. In many towns there had been riots against them. Thousands had been killed. Many Jews had been forced at the point of a sword to become baptized, and many others had allowed themselves to become Christians in order to be free of attacks. However, great numbers of Jews had continued on

A mahzor, or prayer book for *Yom Kippur*, of a type used by the Sephardic Jews in Portugal and Spain. It is believed that the book was made in this long narrow shape so that it could be quickly hidden in a sleeve in case of a raid by agents of the Inquisition while secret High Holiday services were being held.

9

This picture shows an imagined scene where Spanish Jews ask Ferdinand and Isabella to allow their people to remain in Spain, while Torquemada insists that no mercy be granted.

living as Jews and working in the cities of Spain. It was their country, after all. Their families had lived there for hundreds of years.

The Jewish advisers of the court came to the rulers to plead for their people. Queen Isabella knew that Isaac Abravanel and other Jews had been faithful and helpful to her, but she hardened her heart. The decree would stand, she told them. All Jews who did not accept Christianity, which the queen thought was the "true faith," would have to leave the country by August 2, 1492.

This date, according to the Hebrew calendar, came on the ninth day of the month of Av, a day of fast known as *Tisha b'Av.* * This was the day on which the first Temple in Jerusalem had been destroyed by Babylonia two thousand years before Columbus's time, and the

Section of a beautifully decorated wall in the synagogue built in the fourteenth century in Toledo by the wealthy Jew Samuel Abulafia.

10

Jews had been sent into exile. It was also the date on which the second Temple in Jerusalem had been destroyed by the Romans in the year 70. The Jews of Jerusalem were again taken into exile at that time.

Now, a third great exile had been ordered on this same sad day. The great Jewish community of Spain was about to come to an end.

The First Voyage

Columbus had been getting his ships ready during this time and was hiring sailors for his crew. He was joyfully looking forward to the voyage. One of the most important crew members was the ship's interpreter. Columbus needed a man who could speak many languages. In China, which was one of the places he expected to reach, the interpreter would talk to the Grand Khan of Cathay, the Chinese ruler of whom he had read in the writings of the explorer, Marco Polo.

The best man he could find happened to be a converso, Luis de Torres. As a Jew, this learned man had studied the Bible and the Talmud, so he knew Hebrew and Aramaic. He also knew Arabic, Latin, and Greek. Surely, he would be able to speak to the Chinese emperor!

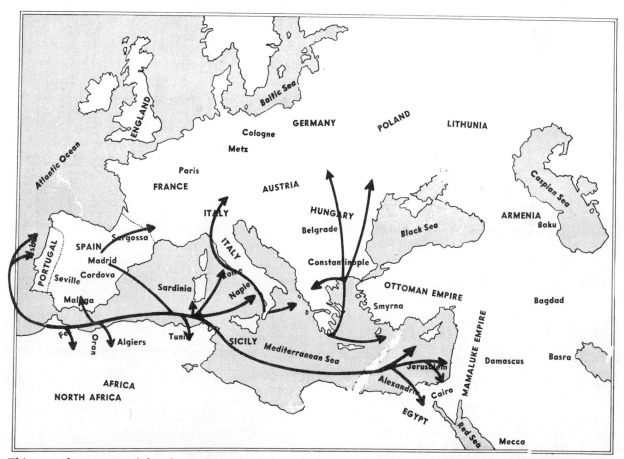

This map shows some of the places, far and near, to which Jews went after the expulsion from Spain. Many went to nearby Portugal, where the Inquisition soon followed them. Others went to North Africa and Egypt, or to Italian cities or further north into Europe. A small group succeeded in returning to Palestine, while large settlements grew up in the east, in cities of the Ottoman Empire.

11

Tab eclipfis luminariuz et primo de fole								
nmer9 annornz	nomina menfinz	dies	digiti	feria	hore	minut	finis eclipfis hore	minu
1493	octob	10	9	5	0	0	1	20
1502	fepteb	30	8	6	17	28	19	12
1506	Julii	20	3	2	1	49	3	3
1513	martii	7	4	1	23	40	1	9
1518	Junii	7	10	2	18	22	19	17
1524	iannaz	23	9	2	3	12	4	6

Tabla de eclipfib9 lune								
1494	fepteb	14	17	1	17	5	2	33
1497	iannaz	18	17	4	3	50	7	18
1500	noueb	5	13	5	10	17	13	30
1501	maii	2	10	1	15	33	19	6
1502	octob	15	14	7	10	15	12	9
1504	februa	20	16	5	10	47	14	13
1505	aug9	14	15	5	5	42	9	6
1508	Junii	12	23	2	15	21	19	0
1509	Junii	2	7	7	9	29	2	3
1511	octob	6	13	2	9	11	2	25
1514	iannaz	29	10	2	14	20	16	3
1515	iannaz	19	15	7	5	0	6	42
1516	Julii	13	14	1	10	0	12	30
1519	noueb	6	20	1	5	50	6	48

A chart from the Perpetual Almanac of Abraham Zacuto, Spanish astronomer whose books were studied by Columbus. The eclipse of the moon on February 29, 1504, is listed.

There were other conversos among the crew as well. Columbus was well satisfied with the two able surgeons on his ships, Dr. Bernal and Dr. Marco. He did not ask them, or his inspector, Rodrigo Sanchez, or Seaman Alonzo de la Calle, if they had been born Christians.

Every evening, Columbus studied his maps and charts, reading the almanac and tables of Abraham Zacuto and the scientific explanations of Rabbi Joseph Vecinho. These Jewish astronomers, knowing the wisdom of the Greeks and Arabs, had mapped the skies to help navigators find their way across the seas.

Columbus and his crew planned to leave at the beginning of August. Like the other people of the land, he saw the Jews getting ready to go into exile. In the harbor of Palos, he saw dignified men and

Most of the conversos were not true believers in their new religion. They secretly tried to keep as much as they could of the Jewish law, and hoped some day to return openly to their original faith. They were called by the insulting name, Marranos, which may have meant "pigs" or "deceivers" in the Spanish slang of those days.

Marrano mothers might light candles Friday evening, hiding them in tall clay jars. Fathers would teach their children a little Hebrew, the blessing over bread, perhaps, and the Shema to say at bedtime. On holidays, especially on Yom Kippur, Marranos would risk their lives and steal through back streets to join fellow Jews in prayer.

women weeping as they boarded unsafe-looking ships with their children. Some of them had paid their last coins for passage. They had been forced to sell all they owned for whatever small price they could get. Their synagogues, businesses

An astrolabe with Hebrew lettering, made by a Jewish astronomer for Alfonso, king of Castile.

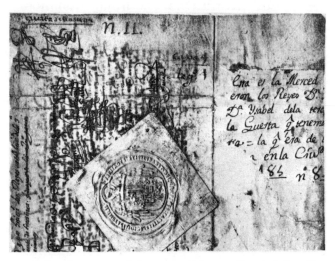

A legal paper giving property confiscated by the Inquisition to a monastery in Cordova, signed by Ferdinand and Isabella.

and buildings were taken over by the government and the Church. The treasury of Spain began to fill up with the spoils taken from the Jewish community.

Many of the Jews thought they might be safe in nearby Portugal. Others hoped to sail through the Mediterranean Sea to one of the Italian cities, or to Turkey, or to North Africa. They could not be sure where they would be permitted to land. There was always the danger of pirates attacking the ships and selling the captives into slavery. Sometimes a ship's captain sailed only a short distance, forced the people off the ships at some deserted coast and abandoned them there. Many Jews knew of such dangers but rather than desert their religion they went into exile.

The last Jews left Spain on August the second. Columbus and his three ships were not able to leave until the next day because so many ships that were loading Jews were in the harbor.

So it was that in writing a report of his trip for the king and queen, Columbus began:

> "After all the Jews had been exiled from your realms and dominion, in that same month Your Highnesses commanded me that with sufficient fleet I should go to India, and for this granted me many rewards."

Following a stop at the Canary Islands, Columbus faced the open sea. He set his course due west. Every night he checked his course with astrolabe* and quadrant,* seafaring instruments which recently had been improved by Jewish scientists.

The new islands, or coast of Hispaniola, which he had discovered, as sketched by Columbus himself in December, 1492.

This imaginative picture, showing Columbus's landing in the New World while naked savages watched and the king approved from across the sea, was printed in a book by Amerigo Vespucci in 1507.

Through five long weeks, Admiral Columbus continued his voyage. The sailors kept growing more and more afraid. Would they drop over the edge of the world? After all, it still seemed to be flat and not round. Even Columbus had not dreamed that the ocean was so large.

Finally, they saw the welcome signs of land birds flying, and of floating weeds, which meant that they were getting close to land. Columbus, awake all night, heard the cry of a sailor. *Tierra, tierra!* he called. "Land, land!"

The First Discovery

A day later, on October 12, 1492, the great discoverer claimed the island of San Salvador in the name of the King and Queen of Spain. He was certain that he had reached India and called the friendly natives Indians.

The shore was rich with trees and plants. The natives helped the sailors find fresh water and fruit to eat. But Columbus would not rest. He wanted to find the

court of Cathay, as he called China. He was not aware that a huge distance stretched out ahead between this island and China.

"De Torres," he ordered, "you will go on a scouting mission. I will expect you back in six days."

The interpreter took with him another sailor and two Indians. In sign language, the guides seemed to indicate that they would bring him to a big place where many people lived.

Only four days later, the men returned. They brought some strange plants, including a weed called tobacco, but no jewels or spices or gold.

"We had to use hatchets to cut our way through the forest," Luis de Torres reported. "We found no one who understood any of my languages. We did find a village of fifty houses, where a thousand people lived, a large number in each house, and they treated us well."

Another imaginative drawing shows Indians attacking the settlers whom Columbus left at Navidad, and setting fire to the fort. The three ships have apparently not yet sailed very far.

"Is that all?" asked Columbus.

"The people of the town brought us with great honor to the house of their chief. They crowded around, touching our hands, trying to see if we were real human beings. They gave us food and drink and presents."

"But the court of Cathay, and the palaces," Columbus said impatiently. "And the streets, were they not paved with gold?"

"Nothing at all like that," said Luis de Torres.

Columbus's face fell. This was the worst disappointment of his life. After the long, brave voyage, his search was not over. He would have to keep on looking for the new way to the Orient.

Luis de Torres, however, was not sad. He had seen the goodness of the land and the friendliness of the people. Like the spies sent by Moses into Canaan, he may have been thinking, "The land which we have passed through to spy out is a very, very good land."

"Sir," said Luis de Torres, "I volunteer to stay as a settler and to help keep the land under Spanish rule when you sail away."

Columbus was pleased. "I will leave

The map shows the four voyages of Columbus from 1492 to 1502. He explored the West Indies and touched the coasts of Central and South America, but never reached North America.

some men here with you," he said. "An educated man like you will be a good governor."

A few historians have thought that Columbus might even have come from a Marrano family. He never revealed much about himself, but often referred to the Bible, and spoke of the ships of King Solomon. He wrote all his records and letters in Spanish, not Italian, although he came from Genoa, Italy. It seems possible that his family might originally have come from Spain, and might have changed its name, as so many Marrano families did.

There is no proof at all that he was ever Jewish. It is true, however, that Columbus knew and was friendly with many Jews and conversos. What is true, also, was that without support from Jews, and the books and instruments of Jewish scientists, he might never have made his voyages.

There is a story, too, that on Columbus's fourth voyage he was captured by unfriendly Indians in Honduras. He was supposed to have saved his life by threatening the Indians with his magic power. He told them that if they did not free him, he would make the moon disappear. At first they laughed. Then, as they waited, they saw the moon begin to black out. Terrified, they untied him and promised to let him go and reward him if he could bring back the moon. Soon it returned. It is interesting to note that Columbus's knowledge of when the eclipse of the moon would take place came from the almanac of Abraham Zacuto.

The New World

Columbus never did find the all-water route. He sailed across the Atlantic and back three more times, finding many islands and the coast of South America. He suffered illness, shipwreck, and imprisonment, but the wealth of the Indies never came into his view. And to the end he never knew that a whole continent which as yet had no name, and a vast ocean on the other side of that continent, stood between him and the Far East.

Luis de Torres, however, had found what he was looking for. He spent the rest of his life in the rough and dangerous new settlement of San Salvador, far from the pleasant cities of his youth. It may be that he preferred not to go back to Spain because there, as a converso, he would always be in danger. Spies would have been watching him, ready to report him to the Inquisition if they suspected that he was still a secret Jew.

Other explorers followed Columbus, and people from Spain and Portugal, and from other lands as well, came to settle in the New World. Among these early settlers were hundreds of Jews, some of whom had been living in Spain and Portugal as conversos.

Many of them were *Marranos,** conversos who lived in public as Christians but who, in their hearts, remained Jews. They had changed only because they felt forced to. In some places of the New World, many of them got the chance to become Jews openly once more. However, disaster overtook some of them. Arrested by agents of the Inquisition, many were put to death, the largest number in Mexico.

Columbus's coat of arms pictures a group of islands, signifying his discoveries. Its motto reads: "Columbus found the New World for Spain."

16

Jews and Marranos were among the many who, hoping for freedom, and a chance for a new life, kept coming to the colonies of the New World. They found their chance in the Dutch, British or French settlements of the Caribbean and the South American coast. Probably the first European to become a permanent settler in the new world was Columbus's interpreter, Luis de Torres.

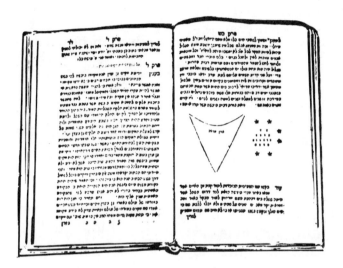

A sort of map of the New World, the first to appear in a Hebrew book, was published in *Iggeret Orhot Olam* by Abraham Farissol, Venice, 1586. The Hebrew words are *Eretz Hadashah*, "new land."

CHAPTER II

Newcomers To New Amsterdam

On a September morning in 1654, a small French ship entered the port of New Amsterdam, the colony founded by the Dutch West India Company at the point where the Hudson River meets the Atlantic Ocean.

The people who lived in the little village, which had been started only thirty years earlier, were always excited when a ship came into their harbor. Ships were their only connection with their old homes across the sea. They always hoped there would be letters aboard the ships from fathers and mothers, or sisters and brothers who were still at home in Holland. There might also be things to buy like cloth and rope and tools, nails and needles. If the ship came from Jamaica or another island of the West Indies, as this one had, there might be sugar and molasses.

Peter Stuyvesant and the Jews

Very important and interesting was the question of what passengers were on the ship. Were they perhaps coming to join their colony? Would there be some new neighbors? What would they be like?

Peter Stuyvesant, the director of the colony, was the first one to hear about the passengers, for the ship's captain had asked him to come aboard to hear a complaint.

"There are twenty-three Jews aboard the ship," said the captain. "They are Dutchmen who lived in Recife in Brazil when it was a Dutch colony. The Portuguese took over Recife, so they left. But they are Dutch, and they say they will settle here. That makes you responsible for them."

An artist's impression of Recife in the 1600s, the wall of the settlement and the church.

Portugal considered the whole country of Brazil as its colony. However, the Dutch conquered the northeastern section, including the port city of Recife, in 1633. They ruled that area until 1654, and during that time many Jews settled there. When the Portuguese drove the Dutch out in 1654, the Jews were no longer safe in Recife.

Most of the Jewish settlers returned to Holland. Some went to live in the West Indies, in Jamaica, Curacao, Barbados, and Surinam, where there were Jewish settlements. One group, after reaching the West Indies, decided to go further north. They had a long and difficult journey, during which they were robbed by pirates. Penniless but healthy, these were the twenty-three Jews who finally arrived in New Amsterdam.

"I won't have them!" shouted Peter Stuyvesant. "Why should I permit every good-for-nothing from every nation and religion to live in my colony? I have trouble enough from Quakers and Lutherans and Catholics. I don't need the Jews here too! This is a Dutch colony, for good members of the Dutch Reformed Church. Take the Jews somewhere else."

The Captain shook his head. "I will take them no further. They have no money. They haven't paid me the full amount of the fare for this trip. They'll stay here and I want my money!"

"Let me see the leader of these scoundrels," said Peter Stuyvesant.

A strong young man with broad shoulders and hands that seemed to be used to hard work, stepped forward. "Your Excellency," he said in perfect Dutch, "I am Asser Levy. My friends and I fought for Holland against the Portuguese, but when the enemy won we had to leave. In order to remain free and to keep our faith, we have come to this outpost of Holland. We will be loyal here as we were in Recife.

We hope to live here as we lived in Recife, and as some of us have lived in Amsterdam, in freedom."

"You may have lived in Recife, and your race may be free to live in Amsterdam," said Stuyvesant, "but this is not Holland. This colony belongs to the Dutch West India Company. I don't take orders from anyone else."

"Then, sir," said Asser Levy, "please write to the Company in Amsterdam, and see what they say. You can tell them that we lost almost everything in the attack on Recife and that pirates on the high seas took the rest. We will work hard to pay our debts, however. Your colony needs workers. We will do our part."

Isaac Aboab, rabbi in Amsterdam and the first rabbi to come to the western hemisphere. In 1642 he was called to the Dutch Jewish community of Recife, but he returned to Amsterdam when the Portuguese conquered the colony and brought in the Inquisition.

The old director, Stuyvesant, turned to the captain and stamped his wooden leg on the floor. "Let them ashore, then! But first, sell all they have. Then, if there still isn't enough money to pay their fare, we'll put a few of them in jail until the others find money somewhere."

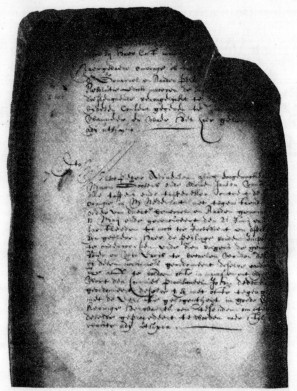

First entry concerning the Jews, in the Dutch records of New Amsterdam, September 7, 1654.

Trouble in the New Colony

"A fine welcome we have received," said Asser Levy to Jacob Barsimson. The two friends sat on a bench that Barsimson had made himself, in the hut he had lived in since he had arrived from Holland a few weeks before.

"No Jews have been welcomed here," said Jacob. "The director had to let me and Solomon Pieterson stay because we had permission from Amsterdam, but he is still trying to make life hard for us. We

There are people who, like Peter Stuyvesant, grow up hating those who live differently from them, or who have different ideas. There were others he did not like, besides Jews.

Unfortunately, many in the world today still act as Stuyvesant did. Hindus have quarrels with Muslims in India, Catholics and Protestants often fight in Northern Ireland, Muslim Turks have made much trouble for Christian Armenians, there are serious problems between whites and blacks in America—people have a long way to go, to learn how to get along with others no matter how different they are.

are not supposed to trade with the Indians, own land, or open a store. You need a license for practically everything and he won't give us one."

"All these rights should be ours," said Asser Levy. "Holland allows them. And in Recife! How pleasant it was to be a citizen there like everyone else. We had every freedom. Jews were even among the leaders. We had a fine community. Two synagogues and our own rabbi. Marranos were not afraid to become Jews once more." Levy sighed and shook his head sadly. "Then the Portuguese had to come with their Inquisition!"

"You must be glad that they allowed you to leave, even if you could take so little with you," said Jacob.

"We could never live under Portuguese rule," said Asser. "We have learned to live as free men. Here, too, we will be free."

Peter Stuyvesant, however, still hoped to be rid of the newcomers. "We have asked them in a friendly way to leave," he had written to the Dutch West India Company back in Amsterdam, "praying that these enemies not be allowed further time to trouble this new colony." And he waited for their reply, so that he could order the twenty-three Jews out.

The answer was slow in coming, since mail had to cross the Atlantic Ocean in sailing ships that took several weeks each way. Meanwhile, the Jews began to be part of the colony. They held High Holiday services quietly in one of their homes, led by Asser Levy.

Peter Stuyvesant could not stop this because the Jews had religious freedom in Holland. But he did do his best to make things difficult. When Asser Levy asked to be licensed as a butcher, he shouted "No!" He said, "No!" when Jacob Cohen Henriques asked to open a bakery. He could not stop them, however, from doing their work privately, behind closed doors. The little Jewish community got the *kosher** meat and bread they needed.

The letter that finally came from Amsterdam did not make Peter Stuyvesant happy. "After thinking about your problem," the letter said, "we have decided that these people may travel and trade in New Netherland and live and remain there, if the poor among them shall not become a burden to the community, but be supported by their own people."

The Jews did not become a burden to the community. Money had come in from Jews in Amsterdam, and the new settlers had worked hard. They paid their debts, helped each other, and soon were able to help other newcomers as well.

The Battle For The Rights of Citizens

"Look at this!" Asser Levy called out to his friend Jacob Barsimson. They had stopped to look at the notices on the wall of the meeting house.

Impressions of New Amsterdam about twenty years after it was first founded by Dutch settlers. In the foreground are Quaker tobacco growers from the West Indies. These were examples of the many different types of people who already lived there.

"One notice says that more men are needed to serve in the Guard to protect the colony. The other one says that Jews can't serve in the Guard!"

"And worse still," said Jacob, "it says that since we do not stand guard duty, we must pay a special tax instead."

"I have been a soldier before," said Asser, "when my colony at Recife was in danger. New Amsterdam is in danger from Indians and others. I will stand guard here as well."

At a meeting of the Council, Stuyvesant was annoyed to hear the secretary say,

"Two Jews with a petition, Your Honor."

Jacob Barsimson and Asser Levy entered. Before they could speak, the director turned on them. "Villains! Where is your tax money? It is now more than two months that you haven't paid your Guard tax. Do you think you can get off free? Should the good citizens of this place stand watch for you and you pay nothing?"

"Your Honor," came the calm, even voice of Asser Levy, "we are men who work hard for a living. We cannot afford to pay sixty-five *stivers** a month. But we

A model of the village of New Amsterdam in 1660. This is very much the way it looked to the first Jewish colonists, who came in 1654.

have offered to serve in the Guard like all citizens of New Amsterdam."

"Citizens! Only honorable men can be citizens of New Amsterdam."

The two men controlled their tempers. Jacob spoke. "Every able-bodied man is needed in this new settlement. We want to do our part. We want to serve in the Guard and protect our colony, like other men."

"Your colony! No one wants you here," said the director. "The other men will refuse to serve with you. Petition is refused."

Peter Stuyvesant was wrong. The other men of the colony were willing to have the Jews serve with them. The more men on guard, the safer they were. At any rate, Asser Levy, and after him other Jews between 16 and 60 joined the Guard of the little settlement without waiting for the director's permission.

The Battle For Rights Goes On

The Jews had won a few victories in the struggle for equal rights in New Amsterdam. They were allowed to buy land for a cemetery, but the governor would not allow them to buy any other property. Salvador D'Andrada bought a house, but was told that he could not keep it. He and four others appealed to the governor and the town council, asking in addition for licenses to travel and trade.

"No!" came the answer from Peter Stuyvesant.

More Jews were now coming from Holland and from Dutch colonies elsewhere in the New World. More letters were written to the Dutch West India Company. Finally, a firm letter came from the home city to the governor of the colony.

The synagogue at the Hague, in Holland, in which the Monsanto family, some of whom later came to America, worshipped.

"We have learned, with displeasure, that you have forbidden the Jews to trade at Fort Orange and South River, and also to buy real estate, which is allowed them here in this country. We wish you had obeyed our orders with more respect."

Stuyvesant wrote a complaint. "There is no more hope of keeping this a Dutch Christian colony. Now everyone can expect rights. Giving the Jews liberty, we cannot refuse it to the Lutherans and the Catholics."

The Jews Request Citizenship Rights

Five men sat in the room that served as parlor and kitchen for the D'Acosta family. It was also the room where the Jews gathered together for prayer services and meetings.

"We have come a long way, all of us," said Joseph D'Acosta. "My family left Spain in 1492. They thought they would be safe in Portugal, but you know what happened five years later. The same anti-Jewish laws and the Inquisition followed us. Children were taken from parents. Spying on conversos was worse than in Spain. It was almost impossible to remain secretly Jewish."

The others nodded in agreement and sighed. D'Acosta continued, "My family succeeded. Finally, my parents were able to escape to blessed Holland, where we were allowed to become Jews openly. And now we are in the New World. Here, we do not have to hide or pretend. We are free to teach our children to live as Jews."

"We have come a long way, true," said Asser Levy, "but we still have much to fight for. We do not have full rights as citizens."

"Right," said D'Acosta. "That was the reason for my speaking. We have decided to ask for citizen rights. Asser Levy, we think you should be the one to speak for us."

"I'm willing to try," said Asser Levy with a smile. "One thing I can say for sure. I know the way to the City Hall."

"Levy, the Jew, is here again," said the clerk at the City Hall.

"What do you want now?" asked the head of the council. "Have you come to pay taxes?"

"Yes," said Asser Levy. "I have come to pay the burgher* tax. I ask that I and the other Jews of the colony be admitted as citizens of New Amsterdam."

"As citizens!" exclaimed the Burgomaster. "On what grounds? By what rights?"

"On many grounds," said Levy. "We are good and faithful members of the community. We belong to the Guard like other citizens."

"That's true," said the clerk, as he wrote Levy's words down.

"We obey laws; we are sober folk. Our word is good in business. We pay taxes,

Resolution of the Amsterdam Portuguese Jewish community granting pioneer Is aac da Costa a *sefer Torah* for Curaçao in the West Indies in 1659. Jews of Holland helped the new communities in many ways.

and last but most important, I have here a burgher certificate issued to a Jew by the city of Amsterdam, Holland, the home city of our colony. And we usually do in New Amsterdam what is done in old Amsterdam."

"Not so fast," said the Burgomaster. "Levy, go outside and wait while the Council talks this over."

Outside the City Hall, Levy spoke with his friends.

"If they say no?" asked Abraham de Lucena.

"Then we can try again," said Levy.

The clerk came to the door, holding a sheet of paper on which he had kept the notes of the hearing. "Asser Levy van Swellem! Your petition is denied."

"It's because of Stuyvesant, isn't it?" Levy challenged him. "You know that legally I am right."

The clerk shrugged. "Go speak to Stuyvesant," he said.

The Jews did exactly that. Their letter to Stuyvesant told of their great surprise at hearing that their request had been refused. It asked why the Jews could not enjoy here the same freedom as their co-religionists in Holland.

The stubborn old governor finally surrendered. He wrote to the Council, "The burgomasters of this City are hereby

THE MASSACHUSETTS BAY IN NEW ENGLAND. 159

into the matters of chardge or answers, as respecting error conce^r Mr Mathews.

1649.

9 May. Voted.

2. Notw^th standing this vote, the house, by vote, judged it meete to consider whether Mr Mathewes, in respect of inconvenient and weake ex[pr]ssions, ... not worthy of some censure.

... the whole C... by vote, that ...

... paid.

binn vsuall ... feitures in s... ... appearance in time, or not so furnished as the law requires in such case, wch the petitioner was ignorant of, have graunted his request, & remitted his fine.

*In answer to the petition of Solomon Francho, the Jew, who requested [*225.]

1649.

9 May. In forma pauperis. Guift to Solomon Franco ye Jew.

ffactorage or salarie out of ye cargo of Imanuell Perada, consigned to the majo^r genñll, Edward Gibbons, Es[q], being by him intrusted and imployed therein; on veiweing & hearing what he could s..., the Courte could not find any cleere ground vp[on] wch factorage should be dew or allowed him by ye majo^r genñll out of the estate of the principles, no estate of Emanuell Peradas being extant; but the Court doth allow the said Solomon Franco sixe shillings p weeke out of the treasury for tenn weekes, for his subsistance, till his passage into Holland, so as he doe it w^thin that time.

19 May, 1649.

There were no Jewish settlers in the Massachusetts Bay Colony in its early days. This record tells how a Jewish traveler, Solomon Franco, unable to collect a claim, was given six shillings a week for his support until he could get passage on a ship back to Holland.

authorized and charged to admit the petitioners and their nation to the burghership, in due form. Signed, Peter Stuyvesant.''

Asser Levy and His Neighbors

One of the reasons that Stuyvesant gave up his fight against the Jews was that he had real enemies to worry about. The English had sent their warships to take New Amsterdam and make it into an English colony. The Dutch West India Company decided it could not afford to defend the settlement in the New World. In 1664, the British took possession of New Amsterdam and changed its name to New York.

It was a good thing Levy had won the battle for citizenship rights, for when the English took over, they allowed everyone to keep the rights given by the Dutch. They went even further, and said that other Protestant groups, besides the Dutch Reformed Church, would be allowed to build churches and worship in their own way.

The Mill Street Synagogue of the *Shearith Israel* Congregation of New York, erected in 1730.

The Lutherans thus at last got the right to build their church, but they were few in number and needed help. Asser Levy, by this time a leading businessman, lent them most of the money they needed.

"What is this, Levy?" asked a Jew, recently arrived from Europe. "You, a good Jew, our leader in prayer, are giving money to help a church? Have you forgotten what the Church has done to us?''

"The Church is not our enemy here," said Asser Levy. "Here there are many small religious groups, not one big Church. Each one wants its freedom. If we're going to ask rights for ourselves, we

The fall of New Amsterdam to the English. Peter Stuyvesant was a determined governor, and would have defended his colony, but the people of the city knew they could not win. He was forced to surrender. The English now controlled the entire coast from Maine to Georgia.

26

must help others gain their rights too.''

Asser Levy bought a house on Mill Street to be used by the Jews for services. "Have we really received permission to have a synagogue?" asked a timid friend.

"No, we have not," said Asser Levy. "The government recognizes as legal only some Protestant groups. The Catholics are still not allowed to have their church, nor the Quakers their meetinghouse. But we will go ahead and hold our services on Mill Street. Once we start, no one will try to stop us."

He was right. The house on Mill street became known as the Jews' Synagogue. The Congregation *Shearith Israel*, meaning Remnant of Israel, which had been meeting in private houses from the time the twenty-three Jews came to New Amsterdam, now had its first home.

Asser Levy was the best-known Jew in New York, as well as one of the leading citizens. He had the respect of all.

A chart for counting the *Omer* between Passover and *Shavuot*, used in the synagogue.

The Liberty Bell in Philadelphia. The inscription on the bell is from the third book of the Bible, Leviticus XXV:10, reading "Proclaim liberty throughout the land, unto all the inhabitants thereof."

Non-Jews as well as Jews joined him in business ventures, and some asked him to take care of their property when the time came for them to die.

Asser Levy built a good house and raised a fine family. He celebrated the Sabbath and holidays with candles and *Kiddush*,* and with white tablecloths and festive meals. Thus, in the still rough new settlement, Jews kept the Jewish law that they had come so far to preserve. Here in New York they could follow it in freedom.

Asser Levy had a son who was also named Asser, for it was the custom of the Sephardic Jews to name children after their fathers. Later, there was another Asser Levy who fought in the Revolutionary War.

For these descendants, and for all the Jews who followed him, Asser Levy helped pave the way for full religious and citizenship rights. In his small way, he helped build the idea in America that "all men are created equal", and that all people should be allowed to enjoy equal rights.

Tombstone of Private Moses Judah, a soldier in the Revolutionary War. He served in the Pennsylvania Militia.

CHAPTER III

Fighters For Freedom

In the hundred years after the founding of New York, the number of British colonies in America grew to thirteen. The settlers began to talk of independence. The American colonists no longer wanted to be told what to do by King George and the English Parliament. They hated paying taxes to England. The colonists insisted that they should have the right to rule themselves. This the British Government refused to grant. Instead, it sent a part of the regular British army to the new land to force the Americans to obey the laws made for them in England.

In Boston in 1770, five men were killed when British soldiers fired at them. Soon after, the Boston Tea Party took place. In April, 1775, Paul Revere made his famous ride to warn the people that the English soldiers, the Redcoats, were coming to attack. This was the start of the American Revolution.

There were about a thousand Jews in all the colonies at this time. Like other Americans, they contributed soldiers and gave support to the Contintental Army. Though there were some Jewish Tories (persons who favored the King of England), most Jews were on the side of the patriots who worked for the Revolution.

Francis Salvador

In Charleston, South Carolina, in 1775, Francis Salvador sat in his lonely room watching the British in the harbor and

This engraving of the Boston Massacre as imagined by Paul Revere was used as propaganda against the British. In the background Revere shows the Old State House, and in the foreground are the victims.

wondering if they would open fire on the city. He also thought of his wife and four little children he had left in London two years before. With all the trouble now, when would they be able to join him in the new country?

He himself was already very much at home in America. His family had been Marranos in Spain and had managed to get to Holland, where they had become Jews once more. Then they moved to England, when that country allowed Jews to enter. And now he was in America where, at last, he had found freedom and the kind of friendship that he had never thought possible for Jews.

He and other men of the colony had met often to discuss independence, and he had joined them in a statement declaring that South Carolina had decided to become a state on its own, separate from England. By a large vote, he was elected to the General Assembly of the new state, the first Jew to be elected to office anywhere in the modern world.

Suddenly he heard shouts from the streets and then a knock at his door. He jumped to his feet.

"Major Williamson has sent word that the British have aroused the Indians to attack the town," the messenger told him.

"We must get our men together and march against them."

Following the plan he and his friends had made, Francis hurried to meet them. Together they started out for the Indian encampment. Near the camp they fell into an ambush. An Indian rifle shot found its mark, and Francis Salvador fell from his horse. Lying wounded at the side of the road, he was scalped and left to die.

The Major found him there. "Have we beaten them off?" asked the dying man.

"Yes," answered his friend. "The British and Indians are routed."

"Then I die content," said Francis as he closed his eyes. He was the first Jew to fall in the struggle for American independence.

The Jews of Newport

It was not only brave young soldiers who showed their loyalty for the American cause. Jewish merchants also helped. They joined other Americans and signed agreements not to import British goods or pay the taxes the British government was trying to collect in America. This took courage because people could be arrested and punished for refusing to pay.

Aaron Lopez, a wealthy shipowner of Newport, Rhode Island, was well known as a rebel. He loved his new country because here he had been able to become a free Jew, after his family had lived for generations as Marranos in Portugal, practicing their religion in secret.

When the British took Newport, all those who did not want to cooperate with them left the city. The Lopez family, the Riveira family, the family of Rabbi Isaac Touro, and all the other Jews who loved Rhode Island now left their homes. If they

Aaron Lopez, distinguished citizen of Newport, Rhode Island. He came from a Marrano family in Portugal in 1752.

had remained, they would have been forced to help the British.

The Jews were sad to leave their beautiful synagogue, the first one built in America. Few of them returned there after the war. Newport declined after the war and was never able to become what it once was, a leading city in America.

On October 30, 1761, two Jews, Aaron Lopez and Isaac Eliezer, both of Newport, were granted the right to be naturalized as citizens.

People of many faiths were attracted to Rhode Island because Roger Williams, its founder, believed in "absolute freedom of conscience," even for "Jews, pagans and Turks."

Among Jewish settlers were Moses Pachecho and Mordecai Campernell, who bought a plot of ground for a Jewish cemetery in 1677. The great poet Henry Wadsworth Longfellow later wrote a warm and understanding poem about this cemetery.

Jewish shipowners came to Newport from Barbados and other ports. Some were interested in whaling as well as

Interior of the beautiful synagogue of Newport, first permanent synagogue to be built in the New World. Named *Yeshuat Israel*, the congregation and its building were supported for many years by Judah Touro, whose father had been the first rabbi.

trade. Jacob Riveira began making candles and soap from spermaceti, or whale oil. Aaron Lopez came from Lisbon, where he and his wife had been Marranos, in 1752. In Newport he became a practising Jew, changing his given name from Duarte to Aaron. He became not only a wealthy shipowner but also a beloved and respected member of the community.

We learn much about the Jews of Newport, their good citizenship and their learning, from the writings of Ezra Stiles, a Christian minister who often visited the beautiful little synagogue, built in 1763, where Isaac Touro served as rabbi. Other rabbis sometimes spoke there, including the dignified Rabbi Hayyim Carigal of

סבטן קדוש ליהוה · יבח האל וערעיך למיז היוה. ני לן
תמיד בישראל · וכזי רישלח את אגרת כתב שלאשתי בתי
הקרב ליהרשלם באר צבי שאלת לה ולביתך בישי לשלום כי
האהביך למענך אהב אני כולם · וישמחו אבן ואמד כעו
תוהר עם אצל קדש ויבקרב רשרפים · אז יבקע הישלי אורך
וארכתך סהרה תצמה והלך לפניך צדקך יבוד יהיה יאספך
ישע נ" ח · ואלה הדברי כותבים בנופורט ראד · אילאנד
לאמריקא כח ימים לחודש תמוז ינה התק לג · אני הצעיר
התלמידי ישוע הנצרי   حمل شمسيل ;

Hebrew letter of Ezra Stiles to Rabbi Carigal. The signature is in Arabic. The Rev. Mr. Stiles loved to discuss matters of religion with Jewish friends, and was a student of Hebrew and the Bible. He often attended services at the Newport Synagogue.

Hebron, Palestine. To Ezra Stiles, he looked like a prophet from Biblical days.

When Ezra Stiles became president of Yale College in New Haven, he wrote the following note about the Jews of that city:

On September 13, 1772 a family of Jews settled here, the first real Jews that settled in New Haven. They came from Venice, Italy. They are three brothers who with their families are in all about 10 souls. Last Saturday they kept holy. One of them fell sick and Dr. Hubbard, the physician, was called. He told me the family were worshipping by themselves in a room in which were light and a suspended lamp. This is the first Jewish worship in New Haven.

The synagogue at Newport was kept in good condition after the Revolution through the money given by the Touro family. It still stands and is now a national shrine.

Haym Salomon The Patriot

In Philadelphia, which was in American hands, there was a synagogue called

Portrait of Hayyim Isaac Carigal.

Mikveh Israel. Among the founders were Jonas Phillips of New York, Michael and Bernard Gratz of Philadelphia, and Haym Salomon. Of all the Jews who helped the Revolution, Haym Salomon is the best known.

He came from a poor Jewish family in Lissa, Poland. While still young, he left home and traveled and worked in many countries. By the time he came to New York in the 1770s, he spoke German, French, Italian, Russian, and English. He had also learned the business of buying and selling, and of handling money matters in every country he lived in.

In the new country, Haym Salomon became friendly with people who were organizing resistance to England. When the war began, the British found that Haym Salomon was helping to get food to the American army stationed north of New York. They arrested him and locked

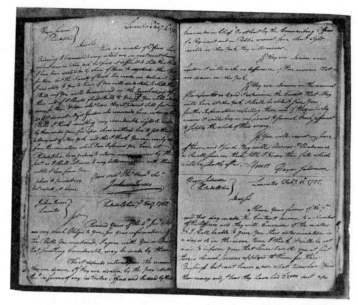

The letter book of Haym Salomon of 1782, showing correspondence.

him up in the Sugar House, a jail that did not even have a roof to protect prisoners from the rain. He was transferred afterward to an even worse jail, where many died.

He was freed after a while for a special reason. Many of the men fighting for the British spoke German. These were the Hessians, soldiers who were sent over by the ruler of the German state of Hesse. The ruler was paid for each one of these men, who were called mercenaries* because they were paid wages for working as soldiers. Because Salomon could speak several languages and knew how to buy supplies, General Heister of the Hessian troops asked the warden of the prison to let him have Salomon as his aide. Haym Salomon was ordered to be an interpreter and provider for the Hessians.

While he carried out orders for the Hessians, Salomon was able secretly to help American prisoners escape, so they could rejoin the Continental army. He was able also to persuade some Hessian men and officers to desert. The British found out what he was doing. When

Barnard Gratz (1738-1801), who with his brother Michael worked at commerce and trade in Philadelphia. Both were leaders in the Jewish community and supporters of the Revolution.

Haym Salomon learned that the guards were coming to arrest him once more, he acted quickly, for this time, his fate would have been death. Without arms or money, Salomon fled New York.

After some difficult days, he arrived in the American-held city of Philadelphia. He looked for and found some fellow Jews. With their help he was able to find work. He brought his wife Rachel and son Ezekiel to Philadelphia. He joined congregation Mikveh Israel, which met in a

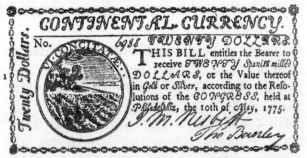

A twenty dollar bill issued by the Continental Congress in 1775. Because there was no real wealth behind the money, the expression grew up that a thing of no value "isn't worth a Continental."

rented hall. He had begun to deal in money and ships' cargoes, and spent his days on Front Street in the business district.

The American army needed gunpowder, food, medicine, blankets—everything. Haym Salomon once asked a broker* he met in the Coffee House how much he was selling his flour for.

"I don't know yet," answered the broker. "I'll see how much the Americans bid. Then I'll get word from my runner on how much the British will pay. I sell to the highest bidder. If the Americans want the goods badly, they will offer more and I will sell to them."

"And if the Americans can't bid as high as the British, you mean you will sell to the British?" asked Haym Salomon. The broker nodded his head.

Haym Salomon was shocked. It was not the way he wanted to do business because he wanted to help the American side. "You are foolish," said one of the other traders. "If the British win, what advantage will you have? You will be considered their enemy."

"The British will not win," said Haym Salomon. "I will stake all my own efforts and all my money on that."

If a business deal ended in a loss, Haym

Salomon would take out his own money to pay back what he had guaranteed. He became known as the most honest of brokers. He would not hold back a shipment of food while soldiers went hungry. He would ship the food and wait for payment. He was not so concerned about his own profit, as he was for the success of the Revolution.

Salomon's Aid to the Revolution

England and France were enemies. When the American Revolution broke out, France took the side of the Americans against England. The French sent men to fight, and supplies for the patriot army. Haym Salomon, who knew French and had contacts in cities of Europe, often had occasion to speak to the French consul.

James Madison, patriot leader and fourth president of the United States. For some time during the Revolutionary war he lived on loans from Haym Salomon.

One day, Haym reported to his wife, who was having a hard time taking care of her little children, "We will do better from now on. The French consul has asked me to carry out all France's business in America. This means that I will be able to make more money, and I will also be able to do more for the cause."

After five years of war and much suffering, the American government and the army were in great trouble. Each state was independent. The states were supposed to be paying their own soldiers, and also the salaries of their delegates to the Continental Congress in Philadelphia. With all farming and business upset by the war, many of the states had difficulty in collecting taxes; often they could not send enough money to pay either the soldiers or the delegates on time.

Haym Salomon, on many occasions, took money out of his own pocket to lend to members of Congress and officers of the army. The records indicate that he lent out a great deal more than he ever got back.

The most famous of the people he helped was James Madison, who was a leading member of the Continental Con-

Robert Morris, wealthy Philadelphian who became director of finance for the Continental Congress and with the aid of other patriots, including several Jews, helped keep the Revolutionary war effort going.

gress and chief writer of the Constitution. His home state of Virginia frequently did not send enough money to support him, and he was often short of funds. Madison, who was to become the fourth president of the United States, hated to borrow money, but in order to eat he had to borrow regularly from Haym Salomon.

In a letter to a friend in Virginia, Madison wrote that he had "for some time been a pensioner on the favor of Haym Salomon, a Jew broker." In another letter he said, "The kindness of our little friend on Front Street near the Coffee House is a fund that will prevent me from extremities.*'" But, Madison continued,

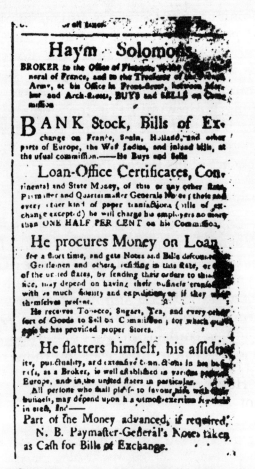

Haym Salomon was one of the chief financiers of the American Revolution. After the war he was appointed "Broker to the Office of Finance." The above is an ad in the *Pennsylvania Packet* of July 20, 1782 announcing the appointment.

Letter from Benjamin Levy, Jewish resident of Baltimore, to Robert Morris, offering accommodations in case Congress had to leave Philadelphia under British attack in 1776.

he hated to take the money because Salomon would not agree to take any interest on the loans. He would not take back one penny more than he had lent.

The Continental Congress had a most difficult time trying to get business people to sell to the American army on credit, because the Congress did not have power during the war to raise much money through taxes. At one point in 1781 the credit of the Congress was so low that practically no one would lend it any money. Robert Morris, then the best known merchant in the country, was

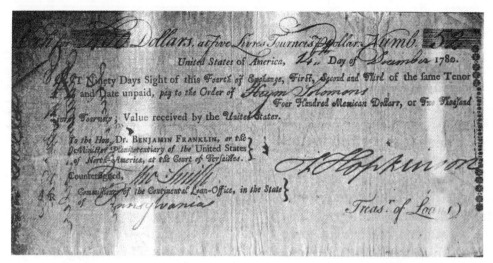

A Bill of Exchange obtained by Haym Salomon. Benjamin Franklin was ambassador of the United States to France at this time, a country that extended loans to America.

appointed by the Congress to be Superintendent of Finance, to take care of all buying, selling, trading, and money matters for the government.

He knew Haym Salomon, but evidently not well at first. In his diary, Robert Morris referred to Haym Salomon in the beginning as "the Jew broker." But soon the diary mentioned Salomon almost every day: "I sent for Mr. Haym Salomon." When a hard job was to be done, or when an officer needed a loan, Haym Salomon was the one who was called for.

Salomon refused to take a profit on work he did directly for the government. He used his own money and his own good name for the cause of independence. He sometimes guaranteed loans made through him to the government by promising to pay back the debt if the government should not be able to do so. Businessmen who were not otherwise willing to give the army goods on credit, did so on Haym Salomon's word that he would repay them.

Many of his Jewish friends also lent or gave money. Among them were Isaac Moses, Benjamin Seixas, and Herman and Aaron Levy. Together they gave many

thousands of dollars to the national treasury.

When the fighting came to an end, Haym Salomon wrote to his parents and family in Poland. Months later he received the welcome answer, a Yiddish letter from his parents. They were both alive, though old and in need. Other relatives in Europe now began to write to the "rich American cousin."

In a letter to his parents (Haym had someone write it for him in Yiddish), he told them "of the joy that I feel on receiving those letters so long wished for." He told them how hard it had been for him "not having any learning." He would not have known what to do "had it not been for the languages that I learned in my travels, such as French, English, etc. Therefore, I would advise all my relations to have their children well-educated, particularly in general languages, and should any of my brothers' children have a good head to learn Hebrew, I would contribute towards his being instructed."

The good son was able to send money. His father had never been able to pay the proper tax for the right to live safely in his home town in Poland. Salomon bought this right for his parents, and he offered to take one or two of the young people in the family and support and educate them in America.

He also found time for another matter dear to his heart. In September of 1782, he had the pleasure of seeing the first real synagogue building of Philadelphia dedicated, the new home of Congregation *Mikveh Israel* on Cherry Hill. He gave the largest donation to the building fund, and also a beautiful *Sefer Torah* (scroll of the Five Books of Moses), imported from Europe. In the following year Salomon served as an officer of the congregation.

Yiddish letter from Barnard Jacobs to Barnard Gratz, 1768.

Helping to dedicate the synagogue were Gershom Mendes Seixas and Jonas Phillips, and the Gratz brothers. The Phillips and the Gratz families had come from Germany, and Haym Salomon from Poland, so that the important members of the Sephardic synagogue were, by this time, not *Sephardim* (Jews of Spanish and Portuguese ancestry) but *Ashkenazim.** Sephardic customs and tunes were, however, kept for the services.

The New Nation

The tasks of the new nation were many. One problem was that of human rights and freedom, for which the war had been fought. Haym Salomon and his friends had much hope and faith in the new country and wanted to be sure that there would be justice for themselves and others in its laws.

However, a Pennsylvania law said that every member of the Pennsylvania assem-

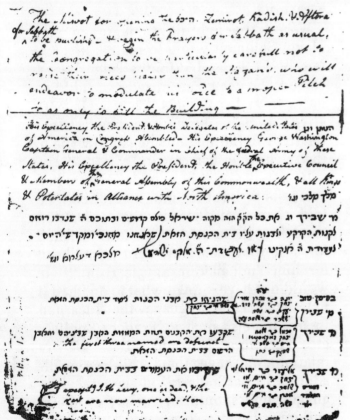

A prayer for George Washington and the Continental Congress. From the original manuscript of the Dedication Exercises at Congregation Mikveh Israel, Philadelphia, Pa., 1782.

bly had to declare, before he could take his seat: "I do acknowledge the Scriptures of the Old and New Testament to be given by Divine inspiration." The New Testament was the Christian Bible, and contained religious teachings which Jews could not accept. They therefore could not say that it was given by God. This law would thus have kept Jews from ever becoming representatives in the state assembly.

The rabbi and the officers of Mikveh Israel Congregation sent a message to the Philadelphia Council. They pointed out that Jews had been among the most loyal

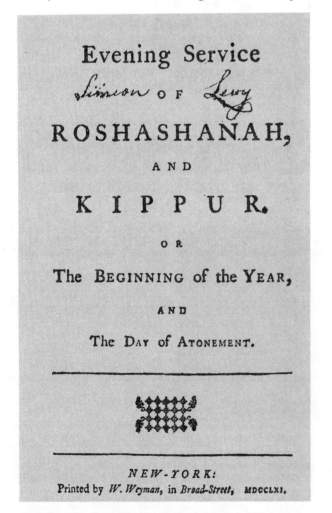

Evening Service

Simeon OF *Levy*

ROSHASHANAH,

AND

KIPPUR.

OR

The BEGINNING of the YEAR,

AND

The DAY of ATONEMENT.

NEW-YORK:
Printed by *W. Weyman*, in *Broad-Street*, MDCCLXI.

The first prayer book for the Jewish holidays published in the American colonies, New York, 1761.

fighters and supporters of the Revolution. This law was against the Bill of Rights, which Thomas Jefferson and other leaders favored, for it denied freedom of religion to the Jews. The letter went on to say that if the Jews of Europe came to America, they would not want to come to Pennsylvania because of this unfair law. They would prefer to go to New York or another state where there was real freedom for Jews, where they could be full citizens.

The petition was successful. In the new Pennsylvania constitution it was declared, "no person shall, on account of his religious sentiments, be disqualified to hold any office or place of trust or profit under this commonwealth."

Haym Salomon planned to move back to New York with his family. But this was not to be. On "Thursday last, expired, after a lingering illness, Mr. Haym Salomon," said the January 11, 1785 issue of the Philadelphia newspaper, "an eminent broker of this city; he was a native of Poland, and of the Hebrew nation. He was remarkable for his skill and integrity in his profession, and for his generous and humane deportment.* His remains were, on Friday last, deposited in the burial ground of the synagogue, in this city. He was forty-four years old when he died." He left his wife with four children, of whom the oldest was seven.

At his death, he owned little. According to his record books, which showed the money that was still owed to him, he should have been worth nearly a quarter of a million dollars. This wealth was only on paper. He had given out so much and taken on so many government debts that he really had nothing. Rachel Salomon and her children returned to New York to be supported by relatives.

The United States government never gave official thanks to Haym Salomon, and few people repaid their debts to his family. However, there is a monument in Chicago showing George Washington with Robert Morris on his right and Haym Salomon on his left, signifying their help to him in the Revolution.

Haym Salomon's love of the Revolutionary cause was tied to his love of his people. He felt that a free America would make it possible for Jews and others who were persecuted in the Old World to be free and live in dignity in this land.

Heroes can be men of the pen as well as men of the gun, men of good deeds as well as men of battle. Haym Salomon, the "little friend on Front Street," as James Madison called him, was, in his own way, a hero of the Revolution.

Chicago's memorial to Haym Salomon, seen standing on one side of George Washington while Robert Morris stands on the other, both supporting him in his fight for freedom.

CHAPTER IV

Jewish Life And Work In The Colonial Period

In the days when the Jews began to come to the English colonies in America, from 1654 on, Jews in Europe were not allowed to do many types of work. The system of manufacturing by hand was based on guilds, societies of master workers that controlled business and production in the towns. A person, after years of training, might be allowed to become a master craftsman, if the guild thought he was ready, and if they felt there was room in the town for another shop in that trade.

But the guilds were closed to Jews. One had to be a Christian to be part of the system in those days. No matter how talented, a Jew could not use his ability to make a living at one of the skilled trades. Jews were kept out of many fields.

It was different in America, however. A person still needed talent and ability to make a living, but his religion no longer stood in his way.

Dr. John de Segueyra, a Portuguese Jew who practised medicine in Virginia in the 18th century. He believed that those who ate a large amount of apples (tomatoes) would never die.

Occupations

In colonial and Revolutionary times, Jews lived mainly in the coastal cities of America and worked at many different jobs. There were traders, shopkeepers, and peddlers. We hear of some who sold brandy, butter, shoes, and snuff. There were butchers and bakers. Some were craftsmen, like those who made soap and candles in Newport. There were also shoemakers, wigmakers, watchmakers.

America's business was open to Jews and many who had the skill became producers. The most famous was Myer Myers, a silversmith of New York, who made beautiful Hanukkah menorahs and synagogue decorations as well as trays and tankards for the general trade.

No. 384
Aaronſburgh Lottery.

THIS TICKET entitles the Bearer to ſuch Lot in the Town of Aaronſburgh, in the county of Northumberland,
as ſhall be drawn againſt its Number.

"This ticket entitles the buyer to such lot in the Town of Aaronsburgh in the county of Northumberland as shall be drawn against its number." A lottery like this helped develop the new town, which was built by Aaron Levy in Pennsylvania.

The talented silversmith, Myer Myers, (1723-1795) made synagogue ornaments as well as items for the general trade. These silver Torah Rimmonim were specially made by Myer Myers for *Congregation Mikveh Israel* of Philadelphia.

Very few were men of wealth. The leading industrialist was Aaron Lopez of Newport, who at one time owned thirty ships which took New England products to ports in the South and the Caribbean Islands and brought back sugar and molasses. His fortune, however, was lost during the Revolution. There were other men, like the Gratz brothers and Aaron Levy of Philadelphia, who became builders and land-developers in Pennsylvania. In the south, there were some landowners, ranchers and planters.

We hear also of Jewish doctors in colonial and revolutionary times. All had learned their profession in Europe. Because some states still had restrictions against religious minorities in the early days, there were very few Jews who were lawyers or judges, in government service, or in other professions.

Moses Lindo of South Carolina was an outstanding planter and trader who became an expert, and served as the state inspector for indigo, the plant used for dye, which was an important export from the colony. The Sheftall, Minis, and Solomons families, among others, became planters. Abraham de Lyon, who learned how to care for vineyards in Portugal, where he had grown up as a Marrano, began to raise grapes in Georgia.

This Hebrew *Hechsher* (document certifying products as *kosher*), signed by Abraham I. Abrahams of Congregation Shearith Israel in New York on February 27, 1767, declared that the Jews of Barbados could safely eat the meats exported to them by Michael Gratz.

Jews and the Early Colleges

The college of Rhode Island opened in 1765. Its charter said that although professors might belong to any Protestant group, there should be absolute liberty of conscience for students.

Moses Lindo sent twenty pounds to Rhode Island from Charleston, with a letter saying that the reason he wished to give money to the college was that Jews might be admitted without regard to their religion. The trustees wrote back, telling him that "youths of the Jewish nation" would be admitted on the same terms as Christians, and would enjoy equal privileges, "and shall be permitted freely to enjoy their own Sabbaths, feasts and fasts, without hindrance." It even went on to say that if enough students wished, there could be a teacher of Judaism or of the Hebrew language. The college's regulations later said that all students had to obey and believe in Christian doctrine, but "young men of the Hebrew nation are to be exempted from this law."

As forty Jews gratefully landed in the port of Savannah, Georgia, in 1732, one of them held the Sefer Torah they had brought with them from England.

Benjamin Sheftall kept a record of their trip in Hebrew, telling how they were twice nearly shipwrecked. When they landed, however, just as in New Amsterdam, there were people in Georgia who were shocked that Jews were coming to the settlement in such numbers.

The newcomers were not sent away, however. A welcome was extended to them for a strange reason. There was an epidemic in the colony. Twenty people had died. There was not a doctor or nurse left. One of the arriving Jews was Dr. Samuel Nunez, a former Marrano who had escaped from Lisbon some time before.

The good physician took charge and "entirely put a stop to the epidemic, so that not one died afterwards." As a diary of that time said, it was like a miracle. The colony was grateful. The Jews were given land. However, some of the colony's trustees were still upset, worrying that Jews would be harmful to the trade and welfare of the settlement. Governor Oglethorpe answered them himself and declared that the Jews were welcome settlers.

An engraving of Harvard College, 1725.

Few Jews went to the College of Rhode Island until much later, when it had changed its name to Brown. In colonial times it was usually only ministers, and some lawyers, who went on to college.

In 1720, Judah Monis had been given a Master of Arts degree by Harvard for his work in Hebrew grammar. Soon after, he converted to Christianity and became an instructor in Hebrew at Harvard.

The first Jew to graduate from the College of Philadelphia, which later became the University of Pennsylvania, was Moses Levy, in 1772. Isaac Abrahams, son of the schoolmaster of Shearith Israel Congregation, graduated from King's College, later called Columbia University, in 1774. Rabbi Gershom Mendes Seixas was made a trustee

Moses Levy of New York, merchant-trader (1665-1728).

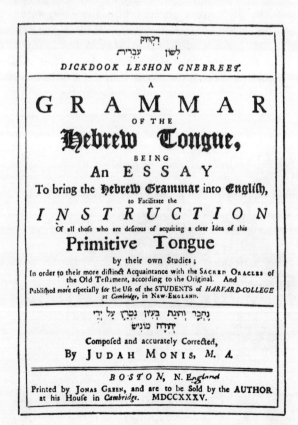

Title page of the Hebrew *Grammar* of Judah Monis, instructor in Hebrew at Harvard, 1735.

of the same college. He was one of the ministers who took part in Washington's inauguration.

Colleges in other parts of the world were not so liberal. Oxford University in England, for instance, did not give a degree to a Jew until 1870.

Revolutionary Soldiers

It is hard to tell how many soldiers of the Revolutionary War were Jews. In every regiment there were names such as Cohen, Israel, Levy, Moses, Myers, Franks, Goldman, which could possibly have been Jewish names. Religion was not listed in the American army records.

Reverend Gershom Mendez Seixas (1745-1816) of Congregation *Shearith Israel*, a portrait copied by J. F. Brown from a miniature made in his lifetime. This picture hangs at Columbia University, of which Seixas had been a trustee from 1787 to 1815.

One of the soldiers we are sure of, however, was Reuben Etting of Baltimore, nineteen years old, who was captured by the British. The records show that he refused to eat pork because he was a Jew. His captors gave him little else to eat. Weak and half-starved, he became ill and never recovered.

There were army doctors who were Jews. One was Dr. Phillip Moses Russell of Virginia, who lived through the winter at Valley Forge with General George Washington.

The Minis and Sheftall families were among the famous patriots of Georgia. Philip Minis, who may have been the first white child to be born in Georgia, fought bravely in the Revolution. His mother, Abigail, helped feed American soldiers in Savannah.

Many volunteers came from across the ocean to join the Americans in their fight for freedom. There were Baron von Steuben from Prussia, Lafayette from France, Pulaski and Kosciusko from Poland. The German, Baron Johann de Kalb, who died in action, commanded four hundred men, of whom so many were Jews that it was sometimes called the "Jewish regiment."

Serving under Baron de Kalb was a young French Jew, Benjamin Nones, who said that he had been drawn by the love of freedom to come to America from his native town of Bordeaux to join the Revolution. He was commended for bravery and promoted to major.

Though most Canadian settlers remained loyal to King George of England, there was a Canadian Jew who left Montreal to join the American army. David Salisbury Franks was arrested for making a slighting statement about a statue of King George. After six days in prison, his friends paid a fine for his release. He left his city and friends and joined the American rebels.

A proclamation of military law in Philadelphia, June 4, 1778, by Major General Benedict Arnold, Commander-in-Chief in that city, issued at his command by David S. Franks, secretary.

Isaac Franks (1759-1822), revolutionary soldier, painted by Gilbert Stuart.

Mordecai Sheftall was called by the British "a very great rebel." When he was captured in battle, a British soldier guarded him with a drawn bayonet. His son, Sheftall Sheftall, age sixteen, fought and was captured with him. After they were released, young Sheftall captained a ship on a mercy mission to bring food to American prisoners in Charleston. He did this when he was only eighteen.

CHAPTER V

A New Nation

The War of the Revolution was over in 1783, and the soldiers went back to their farms and jobs and their waiting families. They began to pick up the threads of their lives where they had left them, but there was a different spirit in the land.

The Declaration of Independence said:

> We hold these truths to be self evident, that all men are created equal, that they are endowed by their Creator with certain unalienable rights, that among these are life, liberty, and the pursuit of happiness; that to ensure these rights, governments are instituted among men.

The Constitution of the new country, the United States of America, and the laws of the individual states, were now supposed to uphold the ideals for which the revolution had been fought.

For nearly two hundred years, settlers had been coming to the American continent looking for freedom—freedom to live and worship as they wished, freedom to work and earn money and support themselves, freedom to think and to speak their minds, and freedom to raise their children to a better life than they had known.

They came from countries of Europe where, for centuries, the poor had worked hard all their lives, but most of the wealth they produced had gone to landowners and nobles. They came from places where they were not allowed to speak freely, especially if they wanted to question what the king or the Church was doing. The common people could not vote or hold office.

The ghetto in Frankfurt.

Religious Groups

Many had come to the New World to escape being imprisoned or killed because they held to religious beliefs that the rulers did not like. Dissenters,* those people of Britain who broke away from the established Church of England, as well as Catholics from Protestant lands, and Jews from intolerant countries, were able to breathe freely in America.

However, there was not complete freedom in America either. Catholics were driven out of many settlements. Four Quakers were hanged by the Puritan authorities in Boston in 1658. The Puritans, who had come to Massachusetts to find religious freedom for themselves because they were being persecuted in England, did not at first give religious freedom to others. In many colonies, as we have seen, Jews were regarded as "aliens" and were not given the rights enjoyed by most of the people.

There is a record of a Jew named Solomon being arrested for traveling out of Boston on a Sunday, and of a Jew named Jacob Lumbrozo being brought to trial in Maryland in 1656 for saying that Jesus was a man, and not God.

From the start, however, in spite of cases like this, Jews and others found more freedom here in America than they had known in Europe. Especially was this true for the Jews. When they started coming to the colonies, their people were not free anywhere in the world. Even in liberal Amsterdam, they could not belong to craft guilds, sell at retail, vote or be elected to public office. Jews had been expelled from England in 1290. They had begun to return in the 1650s, but they still had no legal rights in London. They had the right to vote and hold office in America long before they got such rights in England.

In the German states of the 1600s and 1700s Jews were not allowed to live in many towns. In the cities they lived in ghettos, the part of a city or town in which Jews were confined by law. They had to have special permission to work or to move from one place to another. They paid extra taxes for almost everything they wanted to do.

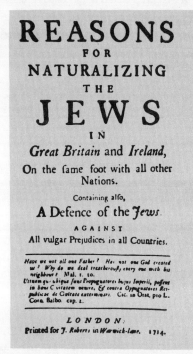

REASONS FOR NATURALIZING THE JEWS IN *Great Britain* and *Ireland*, On the same foot with all other Nations.

Containing also,

A Defence of the *Jews*.

AGAINST

All vulgar Prejudices in all Countries.

Have we not all one Father? Has not one God created us? Why do we deal treacherously, every one with his neighbour? Mal. 1. 10.
Utinam quibique sunt Propugnatores hujus Imperii, possent in bene Civitatem ornare, & contra Oppugnatores Reipublicae de Civitate exterminari. Cic. in Orat. pro L. Corn. Balbo. cap. 2.

LONDON:
Printed for J. Roberts in Warwick-lane. 1714.

Title page of an early appeal for granting full rights of citizenship to the Jews, published in London in 1714. Jews were not granted all rights until more than 150 years later.

All through Europe, Jews were looked upon as a people who were different. Because of their religion, they could not swear in court on the Christian Bible. They had to take a special Jewish oath. They suffered insults and were without protection from the law. They had to depend on the good will of kings or nobles to protect them and this "favor" had to be bought.

We know of Jews who came to America from Portugal; from Italian and German cities; from France; Holland; England, and from the colonies of these nations. Haym Salomon came from Poland, but in the early days of the colonies few Jews came from Eastern Europe. There were also very few who came from the Middle East, which in those days was ruled by Turkey.

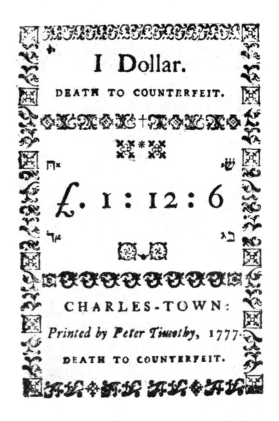

Paper money, one dollar, printed in Charlestown, South Carolina, in 1777, with Hebrew characters as official design.

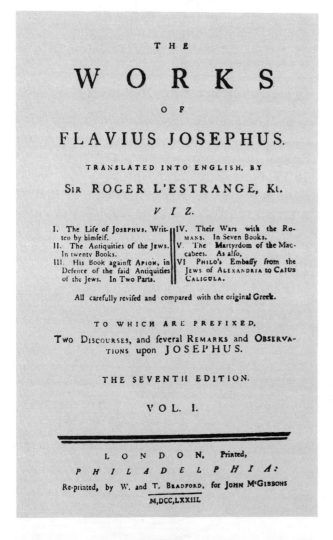

This was the first time the works of Josephus were printed in America. His writings were widely read in the American colonies in imported editions. Next to the Bible, Josephus's *History* and *Wars of the Jews* were the most popular books.

Attitudes Toward Jews in the Colonies

There were not many Jews in colonial America, and yet, especially in New England, there was great interest in them. The Bible was the most popular book in New England. Educated people studied Josephus's *History and Wars of the Jews.* The Puritans compared themselves to the ancient Hebrews, speaking of their own crossing of the Atlantic Ocean as "the crossing of the Sea by the Israelites." They used Hebrew names like Sarah, Isaac, Elihu, Abigail, Ezekiel and Ebenezer.

For many New Englanders, the ideal state was one that would be ruled by the laws of God, like the government of the Israelites under Moses. So great was their

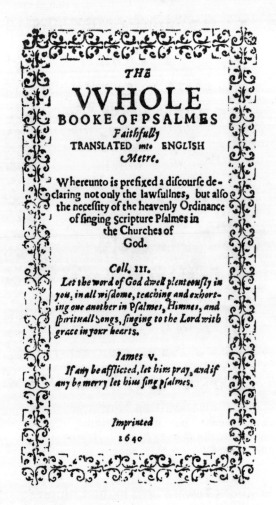

The Bay Psalm Book, printed in Cambridge, Mass., was the first book produced in America. It contains several Hebrew words as well as the rhymed English translations of the Hebrew psalms.

Governor William Bradford of Massachusetts was a student of the Hebrew language. This is the first page of a Hebrew lesson book.

The Jews Before the Revolution

By 1700, there may have been 250 Jews in all the colonies. By the time of the Revolution, there were between 1000 and 1500. New York and Newport may each have had nearly 200. There were smaller numbers in Philadelphia, Charleston, and Savannah. Small groups had settled further inland, in places like Richmond, Virginia and Lancaster, Pennsylvania. A few traveled into unsettled areas to trade

love of the Old Testament, as Christians call the Hebrew Bible, that Harvard, the first college of the colonies, made all students learn Hebrew. The first book printed in the colonies was the *Bay Psalm Book,* a translation of *Tehilim,* the book of Psalms.

In general, the settlers showed curiosity and friendship towards the few Jews in their midst. Some Christians tried to be kind to Jews for a special reason; they hoped to teach them the merits of the Christian faith, so that they might be converted.

This was a suggested design for the seal of the United States, favored by Franklin, Jefferson and Adams. This side shows Moses and the waters of the Red Sea. The American colonists were often compared to the children of Israel escaping from Egypt.

Enoch Zundel, emissary from Jerusalem to collect funds in America for Jews living in the Holy Land.

gogues in Newport, Charleston, and in Philadelphia, while congregations met in rented quarters in Richmond and Savannah.

There were no *yeshivot* (higher schools of religion), or even Hebrew high schools in early America. Some synagogues, like churches, organized their own day schools, teaching religious and general subjects, as did Shearith Israel in New York, since there were no government-supported public schools as yet.

Jews who had learned religious skills in Europe, or from their fathers in America, did the jobs of *shohet** and *mohel.** Men of some learning, like Gershom Mendes Seixas and Isaac Touro, were called rabbi, or sometimes minister or *hazzan.** They were respected by both Jews and Gentiles.

The Jews were scattered through some of the coastal cities. For the most part,

for beaver furs with the Indians, or to sell supplies to farmers.

Jews lived mostly in cities, as they had done in Europe. There they were kept out of rural areas because they were not allowed to own land or become farmers. Some Jews in the new country became farmers and landholders. Most tried to live near other Jews. They needed a community so that they might have prayer services and religious officials to take care of circumcision, weddings and funerals. They wanted to be able to get kosher meat, to pray with a *minyan,** to celebrate the holidays, to have teachers for their children.

In every city they founded synagogues and religious schools, and established cemeteries. At first they could not put up buildings, but by the time the United States was born, there were fine syna-

ז Sajin,	7th.	**ר** Refch *founded* Refh, 20th.
ח Heth,	8th.	**ש** Schin, *founded* Sin, 21st.
ט Teth,	9th.	**ת** Thau, *founded* Tau, 22d.
י Jod, *founded* Yod,	10th.	
כ Caph,	11th.	
ל Lamed,	12th.	
מ Mem,	13th.	
נ Nun,	14th.	
ס Samech,	15th.	
ע Hajin,	16th.	
פ Phe *founded* Pe,	17th.	
צ Tzade,	18th.	
ק Koph,	19th.	

Page showing the Hebrew alphabet in *A Compleat Ephemeris*, a book printed in Philadelphia in 1726. Early America was much interested in the study of Hebrew.

The Declaration of Independence. The famous words "All men are created equal" set the standard for the future policies of the new nation.

they were not wealthy, and not well educated by modern standards. They were, by and large, devoted to the cause of freedom, and among the most willing fighters for independence. They had courage and ambition, and the kind of self-confidence in demanding their rights that the Jews of Europe had not been able to develop as yet. In short, they could fit into the kind of people whom some writers called the "pioneer type," men who were self-reliant and showed a spirit of independence.

After the Revolution

After the Revolution, the people who had fought to free the colonies from England tried to form one nation out of the thirteen free states. Leaders of every state met at the Constitutional Conven-

tion in Philadelphia in 1787, and looked for ways to establish a strong, united country with, at the same time, a guarantee of human rights. James Madison, the chief author of the Constitution, insisted that Article VI should say: "No religious test shall ever be required as a qualification to any office or public trust under the United States." This gave the Jews and members of other religious groups the right to hold any public office in the federal government, including the Presidency.

Most of the American colonies before the Revolution had an "established church," a practice they brought over from Europe. This meant a religion that was favored and supported by the government. In New England, it was often the Congregational Church; in the south, the Anglican Church, as in England.

In each colony that had it, the established church was connected to the government and was supported by taxes. Often, only members of that faith could be officials. Members of other faiths—Catholics, Baptists, Quakers, Jews—would need special permission to worship even in private. They might not be permitted to own land, hold office, teach school, vote; and in some cases, even to live in the state.

The Constitution of the United States did not establish a national church. In fact, Madison and Jefferson and other lovers of freedom wanted to make sure that Congress would never have the right to pass a law that would establish any religion as the preferred one. They worked hard to have a group of amendments added to the Constitution, which are called the Bill of Rights. The first of these ten amendments says that:

The Philadelphia Aurora features an article by Benjamin Nones the revolutionary war hero. Nones answers an antisemitic attack during the presidential campaign of 1800.

Congress shall make no law respecting the establishment of religion, or prohibiting the free exercise thereof.

Thus, church and state were separated so far as our national government was concerned. It took longer, however, for the Constitution of every state to give every religion the same kind of equality.

Thomas Jefferson was the "father" of the law for religious freedom in Virginia. He was so proud of this that he asked that it be noted on his gravestone. In 1777, New York said that "the free toleration of religious profession and worship shall forever hereafter be allowed within the State to all mankind." Thus, in some parts of the New World, Jews lived and voted as full and free citizens while their fellow-Jews in England and in Europe were, at best, tolerated aliens.

Anti-Jewish feelings did not entirely disappear after the signing of the Constitution. The nature of people and the prejudices their families had brought with them did not change overnight. One time, for instance, a Revolutionary War hero and political leader in Jefferson's party, a Jew by the name of Benjamin Nones, was attacked in a newspaper. Unfriendly remarks were made about the fact that he was a Jew. Nones answered this attack boldly in a letter to the newspaper, part of which said:

I am accused of being a Jew. . . . I glory in belonging to that persuasion. I am poor; I am so, my family is also large, but soberly and decently brought up. They have not been taught to revile a Christian because his religion is not so old as theirs. They have not been taught to mock at conscientious* belief.

BY AUTHORITY.

SCHEME OF A LOTTERY

FOR THE BENEFIT

OF THE

HEBREW CONGREGATION

OF THE

CITY OF PHILADELPHIA.

SCHEME.

4000 Tickets at . . . 25 dollars each, . . .		100,000
1 Prize of ten thousand dollars,	- - -	10,000
1 ditto of five thousand,	- - - -	5,000
1 ditto of three thousand,	- - - -	3,000
1 ditto of two thousand,	- - - -	2,000
10 ditto of one thousand,	- - - -	10,000
20 ditto of five hundred,	- - - -	10,000
25 ditto of three hundred,	- - - -	7,500
40 ditto of two hundred,	- - - -	8,000
80 ditto of one hundred,	- - - -	8,000
160 ditto of fifty,	- - - -	8,000
650 ditto of forty,	- - - -	26,000

989 Prizes. Subject to a deduction of only seven and a half per cent.
3011 Blanks. from the fortunate holders of tickets, and to be drawn
_____ in eight drawings of 500 tickets each drawing.
4000 Tickets.

Part of the Prizes to be stationary, and arranged as follows:

First drawn blank on the first day	500	First drawn blank on the fifth day			800
Last do. do. do.	500	Last do. do. do.			1000
First do. do. second day	500	First do. do. sixth day			500
Last do. do. do.	500	Last do. do. do.			1000
First do. do. third day	500	First do. do. seventh day			5000
Last do. do. do.	500	Last do. do. do.			1000
First do. do. fourth day	500	First do. do. eighth day			5000
Last do. do. do.	1000				
First drawn blank, after two hundred and fifty tickets are drawn on the eighth day					2000

THE Commissioners in the above Lottery respectfully inform the public, that they have appointed Mr. Joseph Gratz, Treasurer for said Lottery, who will pay the prizes to fortunate holders of tickets, or their legal representatives, thirty days after the conclusion of the drawing of the said Lottery.

SAMUEL MEEKER,
JACOB SPERRY,
SAMUEL HAYS,
BENJAMIN NONES.

Philadelphia, November 10th 1808.

N. B. Tickets to be had of the Treasurer, corner of Seventh and High streets, and of the Commissioners.

Scheme of a lottery for the benefit of the Hebrew Congregation (Mikveh Israel) of the City of Philadelphia.

Prejudices existed, but the interesting fact about American Jews of those days was that they were readier to defend their rights than their relatives in Europe were. It was not a perfect world; not all men shared the wisdom and vision of Washington, Jefferson, and Madison. But the United States was the first country ever to be founded on the principle that all men are equal, and many people behaved with this truth in mind.

At the parade in Philadelphia, celebrating the adoption of the Constitution, the rabbi of Mikveh Israel marched arm in arm with two Christian ministers.

The Jews of Newport sent a letter of congratulations to George Washington when he became first president of the United States. They wrote:

We now behold a government erected by the majesty of the people, a government which to bigotry* gives no sanction,* to persecution no assistance, but generously affording to all liberty of conscience and immunities* of citizenship, deeming* everyone of whatever nature, tongue or language, equal parts of the great governmental machine.

To this letter, George Washington replied:

"May the children of the stock of Abraham who dwell in this land continue to merit and enjoy the good will of the other inhabitants—while everyone shall sit in safety under his own vine and fig tree and there shall be none to make him afraid." This was a quotation from the Hebrew prophet Micah.

George Washington's famous letter to the Jews of Newport, reiterating their expression of faith in American democracy.

The Providence Gazette and Country Journal.

(Nº 38, of Vol. XXVII.)   SATURDAY, September 18; 1790.   (Nº 1394.)

Published by *JOHN CARTER*, at the Post-Office, near the State-House.

Many religious groups, fraternal organizations, and the Hebrew Congregation of Newport wrote to Washington when he visited that city on August 17, 1790. Above is the letter of the Hebrew Congregation in Newport and Washington's reply.

The Jew Bill

The Constitution of the United States tells how our country is to be governed. While the federal government has many powers, the states were given many rights as well. One of these was control over the rules for electing members of the state legislature.

Some states carried over laws from their colonial days that restricted the rights of minority groups. In Maryland, for instance, there was a law that everyone holding a public office in the state had to declare that he was a Christian and take an oath with his hand on the New Testament. A Jew, therefore, could not legally serve in any state position, even if he were elected.

Solomon Etting, a Jew of Baltimore, had many times asked the state legislature to change this law, but they would not.

In 1818, Thomas Kennedy, a Christian, was elected to the state legislature. He was a follower of Thomas Jefferson, and believed that civil rights and religious freedom should be enjoyed by all people. Mr. Kennedy proposed a new law, "An act to extend to the sect of people professing the Jewish religion, the same rights and privileges that are enjoyed by Christians."

It was surely strange, said Mr. Kennedy, that Maryland, of all states, should not have freedom of religion. Persecuted Catholics had been welcomed there in its early days. "Shall Maryland be the last to adopt a system which the other states, in general, have done and which the United States have adopted?"

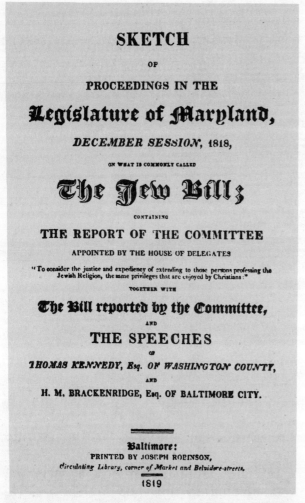

SKETCH

OF

PROCEEDINGS IN THE

Legislature of Maryland,

DECEMBER SESSION, 1818,

ON WHAT IS COMMONLY CALLED

The Jew Bill;

CONTAINING

THE REPORT OF THE COMMITTEE

APPOINTED BY THE HOUSE OF DELEGATES

"To consider the justice and expediency of extending to those persons professing the Jewish Religion, the same privileges that are enjoyed by Christians:"

TOGETHER WITH

The Bill reported by the Committee,

AND

THE SPEECHES

OF

THOMAS KENNEDY, Esq. OF WASHINGTON COUNTY,

AND

H. M. BRACKENRIDGE, Esq. OF BALTIMORE CITY.

Baltimore:

PRINTED BY JOSEPH ROBINSON,

Circulating Library, corner of Market and Belvidere-streets.

1819

The report on the debate in December 1818 of the bill to grant equal rights to Jews in Maryland, introduced many times by Thomas Kennedy before it was finally passed.

The Jew Bill, as the proposed law was known, began, "It is the acknowledged right of all men to worship God according to the dictates of their own consciences," and continued, "Be it enacted by the General Assembly of Maryland, that no religious test shall be required of any person of the sect called Jews, as a qualification to hold any office in this state. And be it enacted that every oath to be administered to any person of the sect of the people called Jews, shall be administered on the five books of Moses."

Mr. Kennedy tried hard to get votes for his bill. "Prejudice, prejudice is against the Bill, and you know prejudice has many followers," he wrote a friend.

When the bill failed by a vote of 50 to 24, a newspaper editorial called it "a disgrace to the state and to the times, a libel* upon the Christian religion." The editor of the Maryland newspaper *Censor* wrote about the Jews: "They may and do fight our battles to the last drop of their hearts' blood, yet they are shut out from the jury box, the bar and the bench! What bigotry!"

Kennedy kept on trying to get the bill through each year. Finally, in 1828, the bill was passed and was made a law, but in a changed form. It said that office-holders would not have to declare anything about their religion; they only had to swear that they believed in justice for all.

In that same year, Solomon Etting and Jacob I. Cohen were elected to the city council of Baltimore, Maryland, and were able to take their seats.

CHAPTER VI

As The Nation Grew

Of the four million people who lived in the thirteen states at the start of the new nation, there may have been about 2500 Jews.

Like other citizens, they were proud to be part of a new democratic country. They were busy and full of ideas, for there was much to do, much new territory to be opened, and every chance to use their talents and skills.

Some Jews joined in the westward movement across the country, as great new areas were added to the United States. There were those who helped build towns, open trade routes or develop business. Some were carpenters and iron workers, and craftsmen and artisans of all kinds. Some entered politics. Those who were talented in writing were able to find success in journalism and in writing poems and plays. Jews were among the many interesting Americans who grew up with the new nation.

Judah Touro

"A noble Israelite snatched us from the jaws of destruction." So wrote the minister of the First Congregational Church of New Orleans. The church had burned down, and the same Jew who had once before saved their building now gave them the complete amount of money they needed for a new one.

This was Judah Touro. His lonely life as an orphan, a wanderer and a bachelor became a good life because of his help to the people around him.

Judah was a baby when his father, the rabbi of Newport, had to leave in order to escape from the British troops during the war. Judah was only nine years old when his father died. His mother took her sons to her brother's house in Boston and she, too, soon passed away.

The uncle, Moses Hays, was a wealthy and respected man. He raised the orphaned brothers, teaching them honesty,

Judah Touro, great philanthropist of New Orleans, in old age.

The church in New Orleans which was later transformed into Sephardic *Nefutzot Yehudah* synagogue with funds given largely by Judah Touro.

concern for the poor, love of their Jewish traditions and love for American democracy that had brought freedom to their family.

Judah Touro, at the age of twenty-six, left his uncle's home and city. Some say the reason was that he and his cousin Catherine were in love with each other and her father would not let them get married. We don't know if this was true. We do know that Judah made a difficult journey to the small, faraway town of New Orleans and that there, among the Spanish and French settlers, he opened a store. The Louisiana Purchase a year later, in 1803, made New Orleans, as well as the great country beyond it, part of the United States. New Orleans became the chief port through which cotton, sugar, grain and tobacco from the southern states passed on their way to the harbors of the world. Judah Touro worked hard and became a wealthy merchant and trader.

During the War of 1812, he enlisted in order to help protect his city. In the last battle of that war, the Battle of New Orleans, he was wounded and left to die. A Christian friend, Rezin Davis Shepherd, came back for him and got him to a

hospital in time. Touro spoke of him as "my dear, old and devoted friend, to whom, under Divine Providence, I am greatly indebted for the preservation of my life."

Though there were few Jews in New Orleans when Judah Touro first settled there, he remained faithful to his religion, becoming well-known for keeping his business closed on the Sabbath. When, finally, a few other Jews arrived and wanted to set up a congregation, it was he who gave the money.

The Battle of New Orleans, designed on the battlefield by the artist.

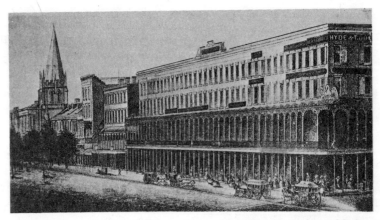

The block of Touro Buildings in New Orleans. Many institutions and establishments in that city still bear the name of Judah Touro, who was a leading citizen and supported many worthwhile causes during his lifetime.

Judah Touro became the leading ship-owner in New Orleans. His ships went as far as Spain and India. He worked hard, living simply in a small apartment, opening his business himself at sunrise and closing it at sunset.

From the beginning, he gave generously to all good causes without waiting to be asked. When he heard that a group was trying to start a public library, he paid all

On March 25, 1828, the first Jewish congregation in New Orleans was incorporated. The Act of Incorporation was filed under the name *Congregation of Israelites of New Orleans.*

the costs for the library building. During a yellow fever epidemic he established a hospital, which became known as the Touro Infirmary.

His brother Abraham was, at this time, paying for keeping up the Jewish cemetery and synagogue in Newport, Rhode Island, even though no Jews remained in the city. After his brother's death, Judah Touro took the responsibility. He also gave money for the library, for the Old Stone Mill Park, and for other improvements in Newport.

When a group of people made an appeal for the building of the Bunker Hill Monument in Boston, Judah Touro gave them $10,000. He gave many private gifts as well. He paid for the freedom of black slaves and helped some of them to set up their own businesses. At one time he gave a large gift to help the Jews who lived in China, about whom he had read in the *Occident* magazine. He didn't go out of his way to be thanked or honored for all the good things he did. He supported an old partner in Boston for many years. The man never knew who was sending the money.

In 1850, Judah Touro gave five thousand dollars for the building of a syna-

Mount Sinai Hospital

Mount Sinai Hospital of New York as it looked more than one hundred years ago.

gugue, where James Gutheim became the rabbi. This was a "German" or Ashkenazi synagogue. In the same year, he was happy to see the dedication of a Spanish and Portuguese congregation, where he could pray in his father's way, the *minhag** of his youth.

Gershom Kursheedt, a son-in-law of Gershom Mendes Seixas, wrote letters telling how all the support of the congregation came from one man. "A plainly dressed old man, sitting in the corner, devoutly engaged in prayer; all the honor he ever received was the office of opening the ark."

Two weeks before his death, knowing the end of his life was near, Judah Touro wrote his will. It is a remarkable paper. It named sixty different people and organizations, Jewish and non-Jewish, giving large gifts to many good causes in New Orleans and in Boston, in Philadelphia and in New York.

Eight orphan asylums each received $5,000. The Jews' Hospital of New York, later named Mt. Sinai, received $20,000; Massachusetts General Hospital received

$10,000. The largest gift for a charity institution was $80,000 for an Alms House where the old and poor could live in New Orleans.

Twenty-two "Hebrew congregations" from New York to St. Louis, Missouri were mentioned by name and given endowments. Special gifts were made for Jewish education in New York, Philadelphia, and his own city of New Orleans. Ten thousand dollars was given to keep up the synagogue in Newport, and to pay a rabbi in case the congregation grew larger.

Like all faithful Jews, Judah Touro was concerned for the "land of Israel" and his fellow Jews living there. At that time, the Jews who lived in Palestine were mainly poor city-dwellers in Jerusalem, Hebron, and Tiberias. Judah Touro left $60,000 to help "our unfortunate Jewish brethren in Jerusalem and the Holy Land," asking that the great English philanthropist,* Sir Moses Montefiore, decide how to use the money. Sir Moses used it to build the rows of stone houses that still stand in Jerusalem in the part called Yemin Moshe, near the windmill.

The Touro Infirmary, endowed by Judah Touro in New Orleans. He gave continuously for health services during his life, as well as for religious, cultural and patriotic causes, and help to the poor.

60

The fifty-sixth item in the long will read: "I give and bequeath five thousand dollars to Miss Catherine Hays, now of Richmond, Virginia, as an expression of the kind remembrance in which that esteemed friend is held by me."

Judah Touro had asked to be buried in the Jewish cemetery in Newport and this was done. The entire community and many visitors mourned as he was buried near his brother and mother, and not too far from the grave of Catherine Hays. He had never learned of her death, a few weeks before his.

A friend had sent him a small bag of earth from Jerusalem. This was buried with him so that it could be said he rested in sanctified ground of the Holy Land. Over his grave stands a stone with this inscription: "The last of his name, he inscribed it in the Book of Philanthropy, to be remembered forever."

Rebecca Gratz, her famous portrait by Thomas Sully.

Rebecca Gratz

Two school girls came shyly up to the well-dressed woman on the steps of the Philadelphia synagogue.

"Are you Miss Gratz?" asked one of the girls.

"Yes, I am, dear." said the kindly woman. "Did you want to see me about the Sunday school?"

"No," came the answer. "I just finished reading *Ivanhoe* by Sir Walter Scott; it's the best book I have ever read, and Rebecca in the book is the loveliest person I've ever read about—."

Miss Gratz had begun to smile, a charming smile that made her, though she was a middle-aged woman, really lovely.

"My friend says that you are the real Rebecca. That Washington Irving told Sir Walter Scott about you and how wonderful you are, and that he copied Rebecca after you. Is it true?"

"They say so, my dear," said Miss Gratz gently, "but one can never know for certain about such things." Then she turned and went into the synagogue.

Beautiful and intelligent, a warm friend, always helping others, Rebecca Gratz was known to many people in Philadelphia. Her father was Michael Gratz, a merchant who supported the Revolution and helped to develop the lands of Indiana, Illinois and Kentucky. Her mother's father, Joseph Simon, was a pioneer in Lancaster, Pennsylvania, a man who had helped open the West through Indian trade.

Rebecca was born in 1781, just about the time the Revolution was ending. She went to school for a few years like other girls of well-to-do families. All of her life she read books of every kind and this rounded out her education.

She was sympathetic and alert, aware of everything that went on in the new country. Relatives and friends saved the letters she wrote to them. Reading them today, we can see how interested she was in politics, in new books, in Bible studies, in the health and welfare of every niece and nephew, and in the joys of every friend.

Rebecca made a home for four brothers who never married. When her sister Rachel died, she became mother to the seven children that were left orphaned. Even a non-Jewish girl, Julia Hoffman, became her ward. Yet she never married or had children of her own.

As a young woman, Rebecca went to dances and parties. One escort was Samuel Ewing, whom she liked very much. But she did not marry him. As she wrote in a letter, "My most cherished friends have generally been worshippers of a different faith than mine, and I have not loved them less on that account." She went on to say, "in a family connection," that is, in living as husband and wife, "I think both must have the same religion."

In *Ivanhoe*, Rebecca, the Jewish heroine, saves the life of the Christian hero but does not tell him of her love. Rebecca Gratz admired this loyalty. "Her sensibility," she wrote, "shows the triumph of faith over human affections." Rebecca Gratz was not willing to marry anyone who was not a Jew.

Rebecca in Scott's book may have been named, as so many have thought, after Rebecca Gratz. Washington Irving, a most popular American writer of the time, was her friend. When he visited Sir Walter Scott, he spoke of the beautiful and kind Jewish woman in Philadelphia, her work for the poor and the sick, her loyalty to her religion. Scott, who knew few Jews, was fascinated. When he sent a copy of *Ivanhoe* to Washington Irving, he wrote in it, "How do you like your Rebecca? Does the Rebecca I have pictured here compare well with the pattern given?"

Rebecca in *Ivanhoe* says that she will never marry. "Among our people have been women who gave their thoughts to heaven and their actions to works of kindness to men, tending the sick, feeding the hungry, and relieving the distressed. Among these will Rebecca be numbered." So, too, was Rebecca Gratz.

As a friend, hostess and homemaker for so many of her family, visiting the sick, comforting people who were sad, praying for peace in the time of war, going to concerts and plays, Rebecca might have filled all her days. She is remembered, however, for other things.

When only twenty years old, she was secretary of "The Female Association for the Relief of Women and Children in Reduced Circumstances." About this

The homestead of Rebecca's brother Benjamin Gratz, on Mill Street, in Lexington, Kentucky.

Philadelphia March 15 [...]

My brother to this day my Dearest Ben handed me your letter to read, and the munificent present of $150 as a Purim gift. I know not how to express my thankfulness not alone for the money but the loving consideration which induced you to remember me at the season of gifts. I will endeavor to use it well for your sake, and if I [...] make some poor heart glad and bless you for it. Surely no women have ever been more blest in Brothers than we have, ye have not only carefully labored to produce means out of the tangled & perplexed affairs of our fathers estate for our benefit, but supported us during a life long period with generous & delicate liberality.

I ponder on these things with heart full

* * *

It seems hard to be so long separated as the time shortens when we may meet in this world — but may God bless you — ever & for ever. Always your affectionate & devoted sister Rebecca Gratz

Facsimile of letter from Rebecca Gratz to her brother Benjamin.

group it was written, "All Philadelphia knows and appreciates their services." She was also a founder and secretary for forty years of the Philadelphia Orphan Asylum.

Rebecca Gratz was a leader in the Female Hebrew Benevolent Society, the first American Jewish women's group. They gave charity and help to "indigent* sisters of the House of Israel." There was a Sewing Society to provide clothes and a Fuel Society to see that poor homes were warm during the winter.

In the new country, there were many orphans. In those days, many people died when they were young because they did not have the medicines that we have now. Quite often, these people were immigrants and there were no relatives in America to care for their children. Jewish orphans who were placed in general asylums were not taught their religion, nor raised as Jews.

A letter appeared in the magazine *The Occident* in 1850, asking for the founding of a Hebrew Orphan Asylum. It was signed "A Daughter of Israel." The writer was Rebecca Gratz. When her appeal got results, she became the first president of the Jewish Foster Home of Philadelphia. By that time, she was seventy years old.

Her most active role was as director of the first Hebrew Sunday School in America, which she herself founded in 1838. Most Jewish children growing up in Philadelphia had no religious education except for what might be learned at home. Now they had the chance to learn from Miss Gratz and other teachers Bible stories, prayers and hymns, and some of the ideas of Judaism, such as the belief in one God and the love of justice.

THE

CONSTITUTION

OF

The Female

HEBREW BENEVOLENT SOCIETY

OF PHILADELPHIA.

◆

PHILADELPHIA: PRINTED FOR THE SOCIETY.
J. H. Cunningham, printer.

1825.

First page of the Constitution of the Female Hebrew Benevolent Society of Philadelphia, in which Rebecca Gratz was most active, 1825.

SECOND ANNUAL EXAMINATION

OF THE

SUNDAY SCHOOL

• FOR

RELIGIOUS INSTRUCTION OF ISRAELITES

IN PHILADELPHIA,

HELD AT THE SYNAGOGUE MIKVEH ISRAEL

ON SUNDAY THE 29TH OF MARCH, 1840, 24TH OF VEADAR, 5600,

TOGETHER WITH A PRAYER

BY ISAAC LEESER,

MINISTER OF THE CONGREGATION MIKVEH ISRAEL

AND AN ADDRESS

BY MOSES N. NATHAN,

MINISTER OF THE CONGREGATION SHANGARAY VAHSHAR AT KINGSTON, JAMAICA.

חנוך לנער

PHILADELPHIA:

PRINTED BY ORDER OF THE CONGREGATION.

5600.

No. 458.

Second annual examination of the Sunday School in Philadelphia, March 29, 1840. Isaac Leeser composed a prayer, and visiting Hazzan Moses N. Nathan of Kingston, Jamaica, spoke at the ceremonies.

There were many problems. There were no books in English that the children could use. At first, the classes used Christian Bible translations, hymn-books and catechisms (questions and answers about religion). These had to have many lines corrected, since they were really meant for Protestant Sunday schools.

Two distinguished rabbis, Isaac Leeser and Sabato Morais, visited the school and spoke to the classes. Isaac Leeser wrote a Jewish catechism and dedicated it to Rebecca Gratz. He completed his translation of the Hebrew Bible, so that the pupils could read it without the special emphasis Christian translators sometimes gave the text.

Meeting once a week, the children could not learn Hebrew or go on to advanced study, but they came to know something of the Jewish heritage. In some families that had lived in America for three or four generations, the parents had almost no knowledge of Judaism. Now, their children knew more than they did. "It will be a consolation for much lost time," wrote Miss Gratz, "if this late attempt will improve the degenerate* portion of a once great people."

The Sunday School founded by Rebecca Gratz became the example for many others in the nation. Rebecca Gratz continued to read, to study Hebrew, to be active in the community, and to hold her job as director of the school until she was very old.

The rabbi of Mikveh Israel, her congregation, speaking to the school after her death, said, "She devoted her best energies to service for the lowly and hapless, to improving the new generation of her own brethren. She loved her people and prized her religion above all else and she decided when she was still young that her conduct through life should reflect lustre* on both. Dear children, imitate her, the venerable* and venerated* Rebecca Gratz."

Penina Moise

In another city, another woman became a leading spirit of her community. Penina Moise, for many years the "Poet Laureate" of Charleston, South Carolina, was born in 1797 to French-speaking parents who had escaped from a slave rebellion in the West Indies a few years before.

The young Penina studied and read by herself. When her father's death forced her to leave school, and she was only twelve years old, she studied more and more. She learned well and was familiar with the Bible, along with the writings of Homer and Shakespeare and the authors of her own day. She and her sister opened a school for young ladies.

For many years, she was the superintendent of the Sunday School of Congregation *Beth Elohim* in Charleston. Though she wrote poetry for newspapers and magazines, her favorite work was writing hymns based on the Psalms of the Bible.

Penina Moise was much in favor of the Reform group in Beth Elohim. Her brother Abraham helped start this group. Another member was Isaac Harby, a brilliant young man who headed a school for boys near Charleston, where the subjects included arithmetic, penmanship, Latin and Greek classics and geometry. He was a writer and editor for several liberal newspapers, but loved best to write plays.

In writing about the Reform group of Beth Elohim, Isaac Harby said, "We wish not to overthrow but to rebuild, not to destroy but to reform." This was in 1824, before there were any Reform rabbis or temples in America. The Society of Reformed Israelites wanted to change the services in Beth Elohim. They asked for shorter services, translation of the Torah portion into English, the use of English in songs and prayer. Abraham Moise wrote, "It is not everyone who has the means, and many have not the time, to acquire knowledge of the Hebrew language."

The members of the group thought that reform of the service would bring back many of the younger Jews in Charleston who were not interested in their religion, and that this would help them to learn the ideas of Judaism. They wanted to have choral singing and organ music to make the services attractive; and sermons to explain the Torah reading. "If, like other ministers, our reader would make a chapter or verse the subject of an English discourse,* once a week, at the end of the year the people would know something about that religion which, at the present time, they know so little," said Abraham Moise.

When Isaac Harby left Charleston to go to New York to become a playwright, the small group gave up its plan to build a new congregation. They joined with Beth Elohim once more, but continued to work for reform.

In 1841, when a new building was dedicated for Beth Elohim, with a new rabbi at its head, many of the ideas they wanted were carried out. There was an organ in the new temple and a choir of men and women singers; the service was shortened and parts of it were translated.

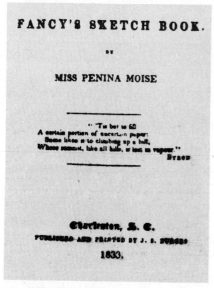

Title page of a book by Penina Moise.

65

The *Beth Elohim* Synagogue in Charleston in 1794, as drawn by Jewish artist Solomon N. Carvalho. The building burned in the great fire of 1838.

The new Reform temple, Beth Elohim, had a ceremony of dedication. A hymn written by Penina Moise was used as the first hymn at the service. One part said:

> Hear, O Supreme! Our humble invocation:* Our country, kindred, and the stranger bless! Bless too, this sanctuary's consecration, Its hallowed purpose on our hearts impress.

> Still, still, let choral harmony
> Ascend before Thy Throne;
> While echoing Seraphim* reply:
> The Lord our God is One!

Her little collection called "Hymns Written for the Use of Hebrew Congregations" was printed by Beth Elohim. Her words still appear in some books of prayers.

The long life of Penina Moise was one of reading, writing, and teaching of religious thoughts. All this continued even in her old age, when, for the last twenty-five years of her life she was blind and in pain.

In one of her early hymns, she wrote:

> O, should my term of life exceed
> Frail man's allotted days,
> In age to Mercy would I plead
> For strength my God to praise.

Penina lived to be 83 years old. Yet, she kept interest in her Sabbath School, listened to words read to her by a niece who loved her, and kept on in her praise of God. She wrote:

> Yet from Mercy's aid shall spring
> Strength of spirit still to sing
> 'Mid bereavement,* pain and woe,
> Hallelujah, be it so!

Isaac Harby (1788-1828), writer and teacher of Charleston.

Uriah Phillips Levy

Not all the Jews of the early United States spent their lives in learning and religion and writing. Some were adventurous and found action in the Army or Navy, or in travel and politics.

In every war, there were Jewish fight-

MISCELLANEOUS WRITINGS

OF THE LATE

ISAAC HARBY, ESQ.

ARRANGED AND PUBLISHED BY HENRY L. PINCKNEY AND
ABRAHAM MOISE, FOR THE BENEFIT OF HIS FAMILY.

TO WHICH IS PREFIXED,

A MEMOIR OF HIS LIFE,

BY ABRAHAM MOISE.

Charleston:
PRINTED BY JAMES S. BURGES,
NO. 44 QUEEN-STREET.
1829.

Title page of a collection of writings of Isaac Harby, published after his early death, with a memoir by his associate in community and religious endeavors, Abraham Moise.

ers. A son of Haym Salomon and grandsons of Mordecai Sheftall, as well as several Jewish naval officers, fought in the War of 1812. There were Jews, many of them newcomers from the German States, in the army of Texas at the Alamo and in the Mexican War. In the Mexican war, David Camden de Leon served as both physician and soldier, becoming known as "the fighting doctor."

The best known Jewish officer was Uriah Phillips Levy. His career could be said to have started at the age of ten, when he ran away from his home in Philadelphia to go to sea as a cabin boy. By the time he was twenty, he had been seaman, boatswain, mate, and had even captained his own ship. At the end of his life, he was a Commodore, a flag officer,

the highest rank that the American Navy had at that time.

Uriah Levy served in the War of 1812. His ship was captured and he spent more than a year as a prisoner of war in England. There followed more adventures, mutinies, piracy, and shipwrecks.

A rough fighting man, Levy engaged in duels more than once. He often had reason to feel insulted. Fellow officers did not want to serve with him partly because he had come up from the ranks, but mainly because he was a Jew. At one time in 1857, he was brought up on charges of being an unfit person to be an officer, by officers who wanted to force him out of the service. In his long plea of defense, he wrote:

My parents were Israelites, and I was nurtured in the faith of my ancestors. In deciding to adhere* to it, I have but exercised a right guaranteed to me by the Constitution of my native state and of the United States, a right given to all men by their Maker, a right more precious to each of us than life itself. I have never failed to respect the like freedom of others.

One of the many events commemorating three hundred years of Jewish settlement in this country was the posting of this plaque at the U.S. Military Academy at West Point.

At an early day, and especially from the time it became known to the officers of my age and grade that I aspired to a lieutenancy, I was forced to encounter a large share of the prejudices and hostility by which, for so many ages, the Jew has been pursued. I ask you to unite with the wisest and best men of our own country and of Europe in denouncing these sentiments, not only as injurious to the peace and welfare of the community, but as repugnant* to every dictate of reason, humanity and justice.

Levy won his case and was reinstated. He went on winning promotions until he became a Commodore, in charge of the Mediterranean fleet.

During the years of his life when he was not at sea, Levy became a wealthy man. With some of his fortune, he bought and fixed over the home of his favorite hero, Thomas Jefferson, at Monticello,

Uriah Phillips Levy (1792–1862), fighting naval man and admirer of Thomas Jefferson. He helped abolish corporal punishment in the United States Navy, where he rose to the highest rank, that of flag officer or commodore.

Virginia. He and his family asked that it be made a national shrine. He gave the government a statue of Jefferson, whom he thought of as a great liberal and fighter for freedom.

Uriah Phillips Levy in his own way made a contribution to human dignity. He disliked the common practice of having seamen whipped who broke the rules while on board ship, and he ruled out all forms of corporal punishment on his own ships. When he grew old, he said what he wanted on his gravestone. It was this: "Father of the law for the abolition of the barbarous practice of corporal punishment in the Navy of the United States."

Mordecal Manuel Noah

In the Historical Museum of Buffalo, New York, may be seen a large stone. The letters on it have almost worn away since they were engraved in 1825. There is the first sentence of the *Shema** in Hebrew, followed by "Ararat, A CITY OF REFUGE FOR THE JEWS, founded by MORDECAI MANUEL NOAH, in the month of *Tishri,** September 1825 & in the Fiftieth Year of American Independence."

There is no Ararat, and the building of a city of refuge for the Jews never took place. What kind of man was this, however, to think about saving Jewish lives 150 years ago?

Mordecai Manuel Noah was the best-known Jew in America before the Civil War. First a clerk and reporter in Philadelphia, he went on to Charleston and then to New York. He became outstanding in each city, as an editor of newspapers, a playwright, a politician, a consul, a judge, an honorary major, and a spokesman for the Jewish people.

President Madison appointed Noah as

The report of some of the court proceedings in which the spirited officer, Commander Uriah P. Levy, was involved during his career in the United States Navy.

consul to Tunis in North Africa. The pirates of the Barbary States often stole ships and took passengers from them to hold for ransom. It was Mordecai Noah's job to deal with these tough pirates, and pay the ransoms if necessary, and do all he could to free captured American citizens. He became a friend of the Bey of Tunis, as the ruler of the Barbary States was called, and during the two years he was there, he succeeded in getting the release of a number of captives.

All Americans who landed in Tunis would visit the American Consulate. One day, a ship's captain brought a note in a sealed envelope, from the Secretary of State in Washington.

Noah thought it was a routine matter, and opened the envelope while the ship's captain waited. His face grew pale as he read, but he hid his feelings from the visitor. Without warning, the note told him that he was dismissed from his post, and that he was to return to America. He was shocked to read that the Secretary of State had decided that Noah's religion "would form an obstacle" to his being a good consul. The note also suggested that his money accounts were not in order.

Noah returned to America and fought back. He published a pamphlet defending himself. He demanded that the government clear his name and got a statement saying that his accounts were clear and that he was honest. However, the attack on him as a Jew made him even angrier.

"I find my own government insulting the religious feelings of a whole nation. O, shame, shame!" he wrote. Proud of his family's loyalty to America—he claimed Dr. Samuel Nunez as an ancestor, and his grandfather, Jonas Phillips, was a Revolutionary patriot—he was equally proud of being a Jew.

"The citizens of the United States who profess the Hebrew religion have merited, by their exemplary* conduct, the rights which they enjoy. Forty years of freedom have strengthened their devotion to a

This "cornerstone" of the proposed Jewish city of **Ararat on Grand Island in the Niagara River**, set forth by Mordecai Manuel Noah, is now in the museum of the **Buffalo Historical Society.**

Mordecai Manuel Noah (1785-1851), writer, politician, and well-known public figure.

nounced that he would dedicate Grand Island in the Niagara River as a refuge for the Jews of the world. Noah arranged a ceremony in a Buffalo church to announce his plans. Reporters were invited. There was band music and the firing of a 21-gun salute. Noah, dressed in crimson robes as a "Judge of Israel," made a speech inviting all the persecuted Jews from every land on earth to settle on Grand Island, which at that time had no people on it. There they would live in freedom, he said, protected by the government of the United States, until the country which had broken down the barriers of superstition in proclaiming civil and religious liberty. The brightest link in our chain of union is religious liberty, the emancipation of the soul from temporal* authority."

Back in New York, Noah continued to write and to work for his political party. Many of his plays were shown in New York theaters. He became Sheriff of New York, and later surveyor of the port, and finally judge.

There is a story that when he became Sheriff, someone protested, saying, "Fine thing, that a Jew should be hanging Christians!" To this, Noah is supposed to have said, "Fine Christians, to need hanging by anyone!"

Noah made headlines in the news with the dramatic event of 1825. He an-

TRAVELS

IN

ENGLAND, FRANCE, SPAIN,

AND THE

BARBARY STATES,

IN THE YEARS 1813—14 AND 15.

BY MORDECAI M. NOAH,

LATE CONSUL OF THE UNITED STATES FOR THE CITY AND KINGDOM OF TUNIS;
MEMBER OF THE NEW-YORK HISTORICAL SOCIETY, &c.

NEW-YORK:
PUBLISHED BY KIRK AND MERCEIN, WALL-STREET.
LONDON:
BY JOHN MILLER, NO. 25 BOW-STREET, COVENT-GARDEN.
::::::::
1819.

Title page of a book written by Mordecai Manuel Noah after the travels he undertook in his brief role as consul of the United States in Tunis.

time came for them to enter their own land of Palestine.

He also invited "our brethren the Indians." He was sure, like some others of the time, that the Indians of America were descendants of the ten lost tribes of Israel.

Noah named the new settlement Ararat because the ark of the Noah of the Bible came down to rest, after the Flood, on a mountain called Ararat. But nothing came of the great plan. No Jews or Indians ever went to Grand Island. In later years, the whole idea was forgotten.

Major Noah did not give up his hopes of helping the Jewish people. He was convinced that the Jews must have their own country in Palestine once more. Palestine at that time was considered to be part of Syria. Like the whole Middle East area, it was included in the Ottoman Empire that was ruled by Turkey. The Jews who lived in Jerusalem, Hebron,

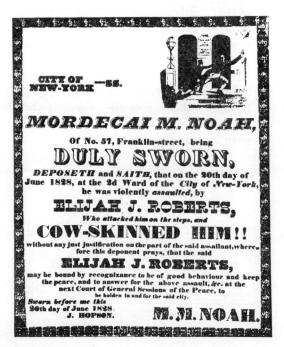

A notice of one of the many public encounters in which Noah was involved in his career as outspoken editor and journalist and political fighter. He did not try to avoid publicity.

DISCOURSE,

DELIVERED AT THE

CONSECRATION OF THE SYNAGOGUE

OF

קק שארית ישראל

IN THE CITY OF NEW-YORK,

ON FRIDAY, THE 10th OF NISAN, 5578, CORRESPONDING
WITH THE 17th OF APRIL, 1818.

BY MORDECAI M. NOAH,

NEW-YORK:

PRINTED BY C. S. VAN WINKLE,
No. 101 Greenwich-street.

1818.

A leading citizen, Noah always placed Jewish interests high on his list of activities. He was asked to speak at many community gatherings, from general trade groups to Jewish congregations.

Tiberias and Safed believed that some day the Messiah would come to give them freedom in their own land. Like all Jews, Noah prayed for the time when God would bring them back to their land and rebuild the city of Jerusalem. But he did not want to wait for the days of the Messiah. "The Jewish people must now do something for themselves," he said. "My faith does not rest wholly in miracles."

He wanted Jews of the world to collect funds for the return of the Jewish homeland. He was sure that the Turkish rulers would be happy to give Palestine to the

Jews for the sum of "twelve or thirteen million dollars." He hoped for the "cooperation and protection of England and France." Almost like a prophet, he foresaw that even Jews who did not go to the new homeland themselves would tax themselves to help their brothers settle there. He was convinced that the new land would be a democracy, an example to other countries.

Mordecai Manuel Noah was a modern Zionist before Theodor Herzl, the one who actually united the Jews to begin to work towards getting their land back. In dramatic words, Noah described the promise of the Jewish State:

Once again unfurl the standard of Judah on Mount Zion. Placed in possession of their ancient heritage by and with the consent and cooperation of their Christian brethren, establishing a government of peace and good will on earth, it may be then said, behold the fulfillment of prediction* and prophecy*. . . . Taking their rank once more among the nations of the earth, they may by their tolerance, their good faith, their charity and enlarged liberal views, merit what has been said in their behalf by inspired writers, "Blessed are they who bless Israel!"

Some Excerpts from Isaac Lesser's

CATECHISM FOR JEWISH CHILDREN

In what relation do we stand to God?

God is our Father, and we are His children.

In what manner can we display our love to God?

By using the gifts which He has given us for the best purposes. To hold whatever we possess as liable to be at all times taken back, when He in His wisdom may see fit to take it away from us. To devote our possessions to acts of benevolence towards other human beings who are, like ourselves, children of the same great Father.

How are we to love God in our neighbor?

We should honor in our neighbor the image of God, and look upon him as our equal and brother, though he may be subject to our control for the present; for the time will come, when death will render us all equal again, and when we must appear in judgment before the Lord our God. It is therefore that we ought to practice brotherly love and kindness towards all the children of the Lord's creation.

CHAPTER VII

Moving Westward

"In general, the Israelites here live completely free and without restrictions, like all the rest of the citizens."

These words were written in German in a letter which had come all the way from America to a Bavarian town, in 1835. The letter was passed from hand to hand by the members of the writer's family as they sat one evening in their small home.

"Is it really true?" asked the second son in the family. The others also shook their heads in wonder. "If Jakob says so, it must be true," said the mother.

"Then I could use my skill as a watchmaker there in America!" said the young man. "Here, they won't give me a license, even though I'm good at the craft. They don't want Jews taking business away from Christians. When I applied for permission to go to another town, they wouldn't let me."

"In America, you don't need permission to go to another town," said the father. "The letter says everyone can go where he wants. You don't need any papers, and they don't ask your religion at all. The government doesn't care what religion you follow."

"They have no reason to ask," said the sister. "The laws are the same for all people. Jew or Christian, it is all the same

An antisemitic cartoon of an English Jew of the Stock Exchange, from the eighteenth century.

in court, the same in living where you want to, the same in voting."

"There is no draft there for anyone," said the mother thoughtfully. "The army is made up of volunteers only. Here, even though we Jews have no rights and cannot vote, our sons have to serve in an antisemitic army."

The Jews' Synagogue, Elm Street, in New York. B'nai Jeshurun was the first Ashkenazi synagogue, following the "German and Polish minhag," to be established in New York. This building was consecrated in 1827, by a group which separated from the Shearith Israel Congregation.

"I could even get married there," said the youngest son. "How can I stay here when the law says only one in each Jewish family can set up a new home— and you, my dear brother, are already engaged."

The mother looked at her children. "I don't want to lose you," she said, with tears in her eyes. "America is so far away. But if you want to follow your brother, I will have to give you my blessings, and Papa will also."

"Mother," said the youngest son, "don't cry. When I have made my fortune in America—and they say the streets there are paved with gold—I will send for you and Papa."

A Wave of German Jewish Immigrants

The New World was the promised land of freedom for millions of people in Europe. There had been revolutions in France and other countries, but many people still did not have equality and civil rights. Unfriendly governments often came back into power and brought with them some of the old-time restrictions against Jews, peasants and others. Life became especially difficult for those who had fought for freedom. Many from Central Europe and the German states began to flock to the American States.

When Jews started to come in large numbers from these areas, there were about three thousand Jews in the United

JEWISH CITY POPULATION: 1820

city	Jewish population	total population
Charleston	700	37,000
New York City	550	123,000
Philadelphia	450	112,000
Richmond	200	12,000
Baltimore	150	62,000
Savannah	100	7,000
Balance of U.S. (scattered)*	500-600	
Total	2,650-2,750	

States. This was in 1820, and most of the Jews then were native-born Americans. By 1840, there were 40,000 Jews, the majority of them immigrants or the children of immigrants.

The newcomers became part of a growing country with open borders. The Jews found communities of fellow-Jews in the cities of the coast, New York, Philadelphia, Baltimore, Richmond and Charleston. There were smaller numbers in a few inland cities. As early as the 1790s adventurous Jews had traveled

Ohabei Shalom Synagogue in Boston. Organized by German immigrants in 1843, this Orthodox house of worship was built in 1852.

alone into the interior to set up trading posts, or to start new farms in such frontier areas as Natchez, Mississippi, and Montgomery, Alabama. John Lawe, a Jew from Montreal, traded with Indians at Green Bay, Wisconsin, and Samuel Solomon came to St. Louis around the year 1805.

Many of the new German immigrants, both Jews and non-Jews, settled in the midwest, in such cities as Cleveland, Cincinnati, Milwaukee and Detroit. All through the midwest one could hear German spoken in the small Jewish communities that began to grow up. Synagogues were started in Cincinnati in 1824, in St. Louis in 1842, and in Chicago in 1847.

Jewish immigrants, like others, worked at many different kinds of jobs. There were some who cleared forests and planted fruit trees and grain, though most of the Jews settled in cities. There are records of Jews, both from the German

states and from Poland and other eastern countries, who became watchmakers, tailors, doctors and lawyers, printers and editors, boatmen and coach drivers.

Many of the Jewish immigrants who came to these shores without money or skills became peddlers. With settlements spreading far and wide across the nation, such men traveled from town to town and brought goods to people. Some walked on foot or rode horseback into the countryside to bring needles and pins, combs and mirrors, ribbons and cloth as well as other welcome things to the farmhouses. Some traveled to far outposts by river boat, returning to their home city after weeks or months.

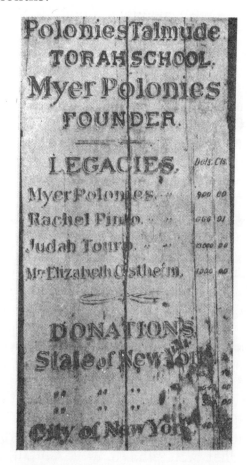

The oldest active religious school in America is the Polonies Talmud Torah of *Congregation Shearith Israel*, which opened May 2, 1803.

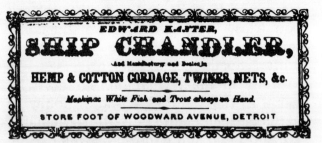

The advertisement of Edward Kanter, Jewish fish-dealer and ship-supplier in early Detroit, 1853.

For many settlers in the new areas, the peddler was often the only visitor from the outside world, and they welcomed him as much for the news he brought as for the comforts of civilization he sold them.

Though they were usually welcomed, the Jewish peddlers found their lives hard. Travel was difficult and dangerous. They were lonely and homesick. They might go many weeks without meeting a fellow Jew or another person who could speak their native language.

One of the hardest things was not being able to keep Jewish religious laws, especially the laws of kosher food. A letter written by one peddler says that he was about to start the Sabbath on Friday afternoon, "unwashed, unshaven, in a Gentile inn," far from home and friends.

The peddlers were ambitious and hardworking. Many who started out with a pack on their back went on to a horse and wagon so as to carry a heavier load of goods. They tried to improve themselves often by opening a store in a new settlement, especially if it was near a road or river landing, which would attract travelers. The store could become a stopping-off place where travelers could rest their horses, and stock up for the journey across the country. As soon as he could, the peddler would keep his promise to send money to brothers or sisters or parents, or perhaps a bride, so they could join him in the new country.

When a few more Jewish families settled nearby, the group would soon arrange for a Jewish cemetery and would try to gather ten men for the minyan for public prayer services. They would hire a shohet to provide kosher meat, and engage a teacher for their children. The larger groups would try to bring a rabbi or hazzan to lead them. With this done, the former peddlers came to feel at home in the new country.

In many towns of the midwest, south and far west, it was a Jew who owned the first general store, selling everything from sugar to flour, from harnesses to hatchets. The clothing or furniture store in many a town bore a name like Goldberg or Cohen on its sign.

Some of the small stores grew in time to be great department stores. Jews were

Levi Strauss was a New York peddler with a pack on his back who caught the "gold fever" in 1850. He sailed around Cape Horn at the tip of South America, then north to San Francisco. But he never got to be a miner. He had come with his pack of needles and pins, string, sewing thread and bolts of cloth. He sold most of his stock in almost no time, and was left with only the bolts of heavy canvas.

He tried to sell some of the canvas to a miner for a tent, but the man said he needed a strong pair of pants much worse. Levi arranged for a tailor to sew up the whole supply into pants, and later added copper rivets to enforce the seams. People talked about Levi's pants as being especially strong, and they went fast. He ordered special denim cloth from France, had the material dyed blue, put a little red tag on the pants he manufactured and a new word was added to the English language: Levi's. The style of pants he was the first to introduce over a hundred years ago is still popular today, and is still referred to as a pair of Levi's.

founders or expanders of such stores as Filene's in Boston, Macy's in New York, and Magnin's in San Francisco.

The Gold Rush Brings Jews to California

In the year 1848 something happened in the United States that caused a large number of Americans, both natives and recent immigrants, to head for the far west. Gold in large quantities was discovered in California soon after it had become a part of the United States. Word spread swiftly across the country, "Gold, gold!" California was on everyone's tongue.

The Gold Rush began in 1849. People by the hundred of thousands crossed the country from east to west, some traveling in caravans of covered wagons and some even taking the long voyage around the southern end of South America and into the Pacific Ocean, then northward until they reached California.

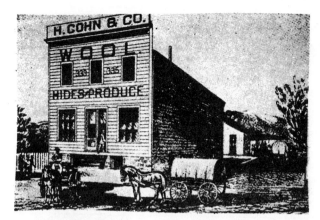

A Jewish-owned firm on State Street, Salt Lake City, Utah, in the 1870s.

Among the Forty-Niners, as those who went to the coast were called, were Jews. Some hoped to find gold; others planned on becoming land developers, merchants or professionals in the new towns that were springing up overnight.

In the very first year of the Gold Rush, there were enough Jews in San Francisco to hold High Holyday services. In the next few years, Jewish congregations started in Sacramento, in Stockton, and in many smaller towns.

Thus it was, that, along with the other

In the excitement of the Gold Rush, all kinds of schemes for getting to California and sharing in its wealth were promoted.

Sutro and workers in the tunnel.

77

A portrait of himself by Solomon Nunes Carvalho (1815-1897), adventurous and talented Jewish artist, photographer and explorer, who crossed the Rocky Mountains with John Charles Fremont's expedition in 1854.

newcomers, Jews were able from the start to help in building up the new state of California. Some became fur traders, miners, growers of grapes, cattle dealers. Adolf Sutro built the great tunnel that carries his name. He was also mayor of San Francisco.

Solomon Heydenfeldt and Henry A. Lyons were elected to the Supreme Court of California. Other Jews were civic leaders in Los Angeles and other cities.

One Jew, Solomon Nunes Carvalho, a painter and photographer, was hired by the great explorer, John C. Fremont, to join him on an expedition* to California in 1853. With him, he crossed the desert and climbed the Rocky Mountains, almost losing his life on the way. When Carvalho came to the city of Los Angeles he sought out the Jews in that community and helped establish the Hebrew Benevolent Society there.

In America many of the early Jews were traders. They rode or traveled on foot bringing goods to wild frontier towns and far away Indian villages. The trader, Julius Meyer (1851-1909) was trusted by the Indians and was adopted as a blood brother into the tribe.

From coast to coast, Jews did their share in the building of the towns and cities of America. They were only a small percentage of the country's population—by 1860 there were 200,000 Jews out of a population of 23 million. Nevertheless it took their work, as well as the work of other ethnic* groups, to make it the great country it is today. All ethnic groups can take pride in the contributions their ancestors made toward the upbuilding of the country.

There is a story that Joseph Jonas, the first Jew to settle in Cincinnati, Ohio, was visited by a Quaker woman from a nearby farm. She wanted to see what one of the "Chosen People" of the Bible looked like.

After studying Joseph's face for a while, she exclaimed, "Why, thee are no different to other people!"

As pioneers of the American frontier,

The first ladies' clothing store of I. Magnin, who became the leading retailer in California.

Jews were indeed not very different from other people. They were part of a new land, learning its language, enjoying its rights and freedoms. Each group set up its own church, and the Jews set up their synagogues. All, as they found their new homes and chose their own way of life, helped settle the large stretches of land between the Atlantic and the Pacific Ocean.

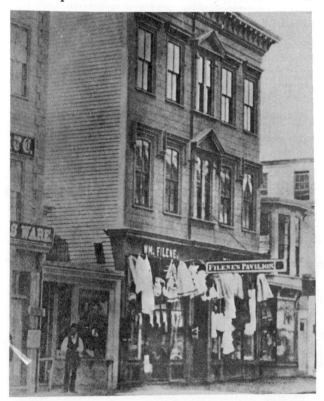

The first small store of the Filene family, who became leading department store owners and mercantile leaders in the Boston area.

Michael Reese Hospital in Chicago, Illinois, named after the Jewish philanthropist (1817–1878). It was built by the United Hebrew Charities. The hospital is still in existence.

79

CHAPTER VIII

Problems

"Who would imagine that such a terrible thing could happen in the world today?" one man asked another. "This is 1840, not the Middle Ages."

"Be thankful that we live in a free country where we can meet together and raise our voices in protest," said his friend.

They were standing in the back of a crowded auditorium in Philadelphia. The man in charge of the meeting, the Reverend Isaac Leeser, rabbi of Congregation Mikveh Israel, introduced a Christian minister, who was one of the speakers.

"I join with the rabbi and with all my Israelite neighbors in deploring this outbreak of medieval* superstition," he said. "We of the Christian faith, loving justice and mercy, cannot but feel shame when a group of people calling itself Christian is guilty of such bigotry."

The minister was talking about the way people of good will all over the world felt about the shocking things that were taking place in Damascus, Syria. In that city, the leader of a monastery* had disappeared. The monks* said that he must have been kidnaped and murdered by the Jews, and that they did it so they might use his blood in the making of matzot for Passover.

This weird "blood accusation" had been heard in earlier times in different parts of the world. In England, in the city of Norwich in 1144 and in Lincoln in 1255, Jews had been put to death for the same untrue charge. In each case, the actual murderers had been able to escape by putting blame on the Jews.

Good Christians were not supposed to believe such lies. Several times, popes had declared that the charge was not true.

Isaac Leeser (1806-1868), rabbi, teacher, translator and organizer, who did much to further Jewish education and raise the standard of community life.

months they were in jail, some went insane and four died.

Most of the world was shocked. But the French, who wanted to gain influence in Syria, did nothing to contradict the Syrian monks, and some newspapers of Europe, a number of them controlled by the Church, even printed articles attacking the Jews.

Jews in America called meetings to protest against the accusation. They felt great concern about the danger to their

A record of the great meeting in Philadelphia to protest the Damascus blood libel. Jews in Damascus had been arrested on the false charge of killing a Christian monk. Jews were joined by many non-Jews in protest meetings in cities of Europe and America.

Jews used no blood in making matzot; they were forbidden to eat any blood at all. One of the things Jews do when they make meat kosher is to drain it of all blood. You would think that such a wild idea would be laughed at, but people heard such stories from childhood on and believed them.

In 1840, thirteen adult Jews of Damascus, including the rabbi, and sixty-five children were arrested, starved and tortured to force them to confess. During the

A portion of the antisemitic report on the Damascus affair sent by the United States Consul at Beyrouth. He believed the outrageous charges. The American State Department disregarded this report, and tried to aid the Jews.

מורה דרך

ללמד את נערי בני ישראל דרכי לשון עברית

THE

HEBREW READER:

HEBREW AND ENGLISH.

DESIGNED

AS AN EASY GUIDE TO THE HEBREW TONGUE,

FOR

JEWISH CHILDREN AND SELF-INSTRUCTION.

NO. I.

THE SPELLING BOOK.

BY ISAAC LEESER.

PHILADELPHIA:

PRINTED BY HASWELL, BARRINGTON, AND HASWELL.
1838.

There were no text books for children to learn Hebrew and other Jewish studies when Isaac Leeser began his work. He published this and other books himself.

fellow Jews in a far-off part of the world. Each meeting sent messages to the United States government, asking for help. The Secretary of State answered Isaac Leeser, telling him that the government had sent an appeal to the Middle East on the behalf of the Jews there, "among whose kindred are found some of the most worthy and patriotic of our citizens."

Other governments also sent notes. Moses Montefiore of England and Adolphe Crémieux of France, two noted Jewish leaders, went to plead the case before the ruler in Cairo. After some months, the people were freed.

A New Kind of Jewish Leader

"It is evident that Jews can come together in times of emergency," said Isaac Leeser. "If only they would unite for the purposes of education and the strengthening of our religious faith."

Isaac Leeser had come from Prussia at the age of seventeen to the home of his uncle in Richmond. He was a student of the Talmud and knew German and Latin. While he worked for his uncle, he learned English well, and wrote articles about Judaism for newspapers.

He was twenty three when he was invited by Congregation Mikveh Israel in Philadelphia to be their Hazzan. He did not feel that he was fit to be a rabbi. He had not been ordained, nor was there any seminary or school for rabbis in America at that time where he could study.

"I would never have consented to serve if others more fitting in point of standing, information or other qualities had been here," he said. The lack of Jewish learning in America became his concern for the rest of his life Writing, translating, teaching, preaching and organizing,

The pass given to the Rev. Isaac Leeser for visiting "the sick of his persuasion" at military hospitals during the Civil War.

INSTRUCTION

IN THE

MOSAIC RELIGION

TRANSLATED FROM THE GERMAN OF

J. JOHLSON

TEACHER OF AN ISRAELITISH SCHOOL AT FRANKFORD ON THE MAINE.

BY

ISAAC LEESER,

READER OF THE PORTUGUESE JEWISH CONGREGATION IN PHILADELPHIA.

יראת ה' ראשית דעת חכמה ומוסר אוילים בזו ׃

" Reverence for the Eternal is the first of knowledge,
And only fools despise wisdom and correction."—Proverbs i. 7

Philadelphia.
PRINTED BY ADAM WALDIE.

Isaac Leeser translated the Bible and prayerbook into English, and also instructive works such as these, for the use of American Jews.

he tried to bring strength to the American Jewish community. He was concerned with American Jews who were moving away from traditional Jewish law, and those who were ready to leave their people completely.

In his sermons and in his writings, he tried to convince Jews that they must be true to their tradition. They were, he said, "guardians of the sacred fire." He published many books to help American Jews learn about their tradition. He put out prayer books with English translations, according to both the Portuguese and the German minhag. For children, especially

those who went to the Sunday School where Rebecca Gratz taught, he prepared a Hebrew spelling book and a Jewish catechism.

For twenty-five years, Isaac Leeser edited and wrote for a monthly magazine, *The Occident.* In it, besides news, were essays, poems, novels, letters from readers and discussions on Jewish religion. Articles told about Jewish congregations not only in the United States but in the Papal States of Italy, in England, in St. Thomas, even in Australia and New Zealand. Many of the write-ups of Jews in American cities were done by Leeser himself, for he visited a great many

THE OCCIDENT,

AND

AMERICAN JEWISH ADVOCATE.

A MONTHLY PERIODICAL

DEVOTED TO

THE DIFFUSION OF KNOWLEDGE

ON

Jewish Literature and Religion.

EDITED

BY ISAAC LEESER.

ללמוד וללמד לשמור ולעשות
" To learn and to teach, to observe and to do."

VOL. I.

PHILADELPHIA:
PUBLISHED AT 118 SOUTH FOURTH STREET.

For 25 years, Isaac Leeser edited and published *The Occident*, leading Jewish periodical, which gave its readers essays, stories and poems, and news of Jewish communities all over the world.

communities. In each city he spoke to rabbis and teachers, and always visited the children in their religious school.

There were often notices in the magazine that a new hazzan or Hebrew teacher or shohet was needed somewhere. There were appeals for money to rebuild a synagogue which had been destroyed by fire, or to help support Jewish schools in Egypt or China and other far-off places.

Another New Jewish Leader

An issue of the *Occident* in 1846 had a small item in it, announcing that Isaac Mayer Wise, a Jew "having some learning," had arrived in New York with his family. Isaac Leeser traveled to Albany the next year to visit Rabbi Wise at his congregation. For many years afterwards, there were discussions between Wise and Leeser, both in person and in print. The two had different ideas about how to be a good Jew, but both wanted to get American Jews together, and to strengthen their Jewish faith and knowledge.

It was not too difficult to bring Jews together when there was some crisis, when they needed to fight anti-Jewish prejudice. Ten years after the Damascus case, for instance, came the news that a treaty was being discussed between the United States and Switzerland, which was intended to open up each country to the citizens of the other country for travel and business. But it accepted a peculiar situation, that those parts of Switzerland that did not allow Jewish residents could keep out American Jews. This meant the United States would not be treating its own Jewish citizens as people worthy of full protection of their government.

Some American leaders, including Daniel Webster and Henry Clay, objected,

but the treaty was signed. Jews met together in Baltimore, Cleveland, Chicago and Cincinnati. Isaac Mayer Wise headed a committee that went to the President, who agreed that it was not a good treaty. It should have assured Jews of the same rights and protection as other American citizens.

Things did not change, however, until some years later. The American government tried to persuade the Swiss government to give rights to its own Jewish citizens. President Lincoln even appointed a Jew as consul to Zurich, Switzerland. Swiss Jews were eventually given the same rights as others in their country. There was no need after that to change the treaty.

It was encouraging to find Jews in America ready to come together in defense of their rights. But Isaac Leeser and

Henry Jones, a founder of B'nai B'rith, largest of Jewish fraternal orders, in 1843, from a drawing by George D. M. Peixotto.

This drawing by Moritz Oppenheim shows the kidnaping of six-year-old Edgar Mortara from his home in Italy in 1858. Papal guards seized him on orders from the Church that the child must be brought up as a Catholic.

Isaac Mayer Wise wanted to see the Jews establish a national Jewish organization that would be active in Jewish causes all year round. They wrote articles and made speeches calling for Jews to join together. They did get representatives to come to a meeting in Cleveland in 1855, but no organization came out of it.

Though Jews were not ready to join in a national union, they were concerned about their people. In every town, they formed groups to take care of the poor and the orphans. In 1843, when there were over 40,000 Jews in the country, the Independent Order of B'nai B'rith was formed and soon after, the Free Sons of Israel.

A shock which again brought the Jews of the country more closely together was the Mortara Case of 1858. A six-year-old Jewish boy who lived in the city of Bologna, in an area ruled by the Pope, was taken away from his home by Papal

In spite of mass meetings such as this one held in San Francisco, addressed by leading citizens both Jewish and non-Jewish, Edgar Mortara was never returned to his parents.

guards and brought to a convent to be raised as a Catholic. His parents never saw Edgar Mortara again. The boy's nurse, a Catholic, had secretly baptized him as a Catholic when he was ill. This meant that in the eyes of the Church he was a Catholic and had to be raised that way.

Meetings were called. Over 2,000 met in New York and 3,000 in San Francisco. Protestant leaders and many newspapers joined in the protest. However, this time the President of the United States did not do anything because, as he said, it was an internal matter in another country.

The Mortara case had a great effect in getting Jews to work for self-defense and the emancipation* of their brothers. The Alliance Israélite Universelle was just being started in France at this time. In

Notice of appointment to the committee to found Maimonides Rabbinical College in Philadelphia, 1864. Isaac Leeser was the leader in this endeavor. The meeting was at the office of Moses Dropsie, who later established Dropsie University.

The Rev. Samuel M. Isaacs of New York. He led congregations B'nai Jeshurun and Shaaray Tefilah. In 1857 he founded the first Jewish weekly, *The Jewish Messenger*, which advocated traditional Judaism and supported abolition of slavery.

England, the British Board of Deputies became more active.

In the United States, a "Board of Delegates of American Israelites" was started in 1859. Delegates came from congregations in thirteen cities and met under the leadership of Rabbi Samuel Isaacs in New York. Isaac Leeser, who had called the meeting, was vice-president. Though a number of other congregations did not join, it was the first group to represent American Jews nationally.

Isaac Leeser continued to try to raise the level of Jewish life in America. He worked for Hebrew schools, Jewish hospitals, and a society to publish Jewish books. His greatest hope was to start a school for higher Jewish studies, which he finally did in 1867. He started Maimonides College in Philadelphia as a seminary* to prepare rabbis and teachers. Unfortunately, it lasted only a few years; it had to close because there were not enough students and there was a lack of money to support the college.

Many of Leeser's ideas were a little ahead of his times. What he worked for came into being after him. He devoted his whole life to the Jewish people. He had no other interests and no family of his own. He wanted his people to love Jewish tradition as he did, and to live according to Jewish law and ideals. He did his best to teach them, and to unite them to work together for Jewish learning as well as for Jewish rights.

CHAPTER IX

Civil War

"I cannot leave the city," said the rabbi. "That would be deserting my post."

One of the men sitting with Rabbi David Einhorn leaned forward earnestly. "Haven't you heard that the printing company that prints your newspaper has been burned?" he asked the rabbi. "If men who are for slavery will destroy a press for printing editorials against slavery, they may also do harm to the writer of these ideas."

"Everyone knows you have been preaching abolition,*" said the second man. "You are well known in this city as an enemy of states' rights. I think you are a marked man, Rabbi."

"But I cannot run away," said Rabbi Einhorn. "I believe in the Union. I am against states breaking it by seceding from the United States. And I feel that it is part of my Jewish faith to be against slavery. I intend to stay here in Baltimore and show that I stick to my beliefs."

The two members of Congregation Har Sinai had come to see their rabbi, David Einhorn, on an April afternoon in 1861. It was a time of trouble. The Civil War was beginning and the Southern states were seceding.* Northerners were trying to

Rabbi David Einhorn (1809-1879), radical Reform leader and outspoken abolitionist, who served pulpits in Philadelphia and New York after leaving Baltimore at the time of pro-slavery riots.

keep the Union together. Violence had broken out in Baltimore which was between the North and the South. Federal troops had been attacked and had fired back. There had been days and nights of riots.

"Please, Rabbi," pleaded one of the men, "for your safety and for ours, go away for a while, just until the violence blows over. While you are here, you make it seem as if all the Jews are abolitionists and against the Confederacy. You must leave Baltimore. Your sermons make trouble for all of us."

Rabbi Einhorn stood up, "If those are the terms on which the congregation will let me stay, on condition that I stop making trouble, that I stop preaching that all men are equally children of God, then I certainly will not stay," he said. "I left Austria because there was no right of free speech there."

"We don't mean to stop your sermons," said the member quickly. "We are only thinking of your safety."

Rabbi Einhorn would have stayed on to lead the fight against slavery but a few days later burning and looting started up in the city. He was in danger of being attacked. Some young Jews armed with guns came to stand guard over the rabbi's house, and he and his family left for Philadelphia.

Sketch from an old newspaper of Arab slave traders looking over captured Africans, who will be transported and sold in America.

Among Jews who worked for abolition was Moritz Pinner, who left Germany after the 1848 revolution. He edited the *Kansas Post,* a newspaper that tried to make Kansas a free state. This was dangerous because there was a gang called "border ruffians," made up of people who wanted Kansas to be a slave state, and who made attacks upon those who were against slavery. Pinner was a delegate to the Republican Party convention in 1860 which nominated Abraham Lincoln for the presidency. He later refused a government post that would have taken him to Honduras; he wanted to fight for the Union instead.

Jews And The Question Of Slavery

It was not true that all Jews were abolitionists. Like other Americans, Jews tended to feel like the people in the part of the country in which they lived. Most Jews living in the South were in favor of the Confederacy; those in the North fought for the Union. Many Jews, however, had been active in the anti-slavery movement years before the war broke out.

August Bondi (1833-1907), abolitionist. After leaving Austria following the 1848 revolution, he, with Jacob Benjamin and Theodore Weiner, joined John Brown's anti-slavery army in Kansas.

Rabbi Morris J. Raphall of New York (1798-1868), scholar, translator and preacher formerly of Stockholm and of England. He was rabbi of B'nai Jeshurun for many years. One of his widely debated talks was on the biblical attitude towards slavery.

One reason for this was the traditional Jewish love of freedom. Jews celebrate their escape from slavery in Egypt every year at Passover. Many Jews who came to America had taken part in revolutions in Europe that aimed to bring liberty to the people. They could not side with those who supported slavery in America. When a mob freed a captured runaway slave in Chicago in 1853, the leader was Michael Greenebaum, one of the first Jews to have settled in that city. Three Jewish immigrants, August Bondi of Vienna, Jacob Benjamin of Bohemia, and Theodore Weiner of Poland, went with John Brown, to fight to keep Kansas from becoming a slave state.

There was a rabbi, Morris Raphall, who defended slavery, provided the masters were kind. Most rabbis, however, spoke out against the evil of slavery. Bernard Felsenthal of Chicago said that most American Jews were "heart and soul

90

dedicated to the anti-slavery movement."
Sabato Morais, rabbi of Mikveh Israel in
Philadelphia after Isaac Leeser, was
warned by his board of trustees to stop
praising Lincoln. Other members, however, said he should preach what he
believed.

When the war broke out, thousands of
Jews in the north joined up. It is not
possible to know how many Jews fought
in the Civil War because the religion of
the soldiers was not listed. A study was
made of all the records in later years of
Jews who fought on the Union side. Over
6,000 Jews were listed.

There were many thousands also on the
Confederate side. The South's Secretary
of War, at one point, declared that he
could not give furloughs to the Jewish
soldiers for the High Holydays, since
there were so many Jews; he claimed
10,000.

Judah P. Benjamin (1811-1884), Confederate statesman. A
senator from Louisiana, he became Attorney-General of
the Confederacy, acting Secretary of War, and Secretary
of State. He fled to England after the war.

Army Jews.

The following co-religionists were either
killed or wounded at the battle of Fredericksburg :

T. J. Heffernam, A, 163 N. Y., hip and arm.
Serg. F. Herrfukneckt, 7 " head.
M. Ellis, 23 N. J., hand.
Moses Steinburg, 142 Penn., legs bruised.
A. Newman, A, 72 " ankle
Lt. H. T. Davis, 81 " arm.
J. Killenback, 4 N. J., head.
S. S. Vanuess, 15 " leg.
W. Truax, 23 " back.
J. Hirsh, 4 " "
Jacob Schmidt, 19 Penn., left arm.
Jos. Osback, 19 " wounded.
W. Jabob, 19 " left arm.
Lieut. Simpson, 19 " left leg.
Capt. Schuh, 19 " wounded.
C. M. Phillips, 16 Maine, cheek.
Lieut. S. Simpson, 99 Penn., leg.
R. Harris, 107 " thigh.

A partial list of Jewish Union Soldiers felled in the
Battle of Fredericksburg, December 13, 1862. In this
battle the Union Army was defeated and suffered over
10,000 casualties in killed and wounded.

Most important of the Jews in the
Confederacy was Judah Philip Benjamin
of Louisiana. He had been a senator from
his state, and left Washington when
Louisiana seceded. He was at one time
Attorney General in the Confederate
government, then the Secretary of War,
and later, Secretary of State. Although he
did not regard himself any longer to be a
Jew, he was so considered by his enemies
on both sides. A northerner called him
"an Israelite with Egyptian principles."
When the South began to lose battles,
some in the Confederacy blamed him

List of Soldiers of the Confederate army buried by George Jacobs. Richmond Va

Names	Regiment &c	Date of interment	Remarks
Henry Cohen	— S C	30th June 1862	Killed in Battle
Edwin Ferson	— Texas	16 July 1862	Killed in battle, 27 June
Jacob A. Cohn	12 Louisiana Rg	29 Sept 1862	" " " " 30 Aug
Lewis Lipman	5 " "	2 may 1863	Died of wound 1 may 1863
Isaac J. Levy	46 Va "	23 Aug 1864	Killed in battle 21 Aug 64
Dan'l Levy	— " "	9 Feby 1866	died of Disease contracted

Richmond Va, May 17th 1866.

Mrs R. C. Levy.

Cor. Sec. Heb. Ladies Association &c.

Madame,

Above I hand you the list of Soldiers buried by me during the late war, as requested by the association, on your letter of 16th inst.

Very respectfully Yours

Geor Jacobs

A list of the Confederate soldiers buried by the Rev. George Jacobs. He sent it to Mrs. R.C. Levy of Richmond, who had requested it. The false accusation was often made that few Jews served in the Civil War; it was disproved by gathering of names such as these.

Leopold Karpeles, awarded the Congressional Medal of Honor for bravery at the Battle of the Wilderness, as color-sergeant of the 57th Massachusetts Infantry.

more than anyone else. After the war, he escaped to England and became a lawyer there.

Suffering as much as the rest of the people on both sides of the battle, the

The Know-Nothing party, with a platform of bigotry, was a powerful group for many years. They hated minority groups, including all recent immigrants. They charged that Irish and German immigrants were stealing American elections and running the big city political machines.

Jews also had to suffer the ill will of antisemites. During hard times, prejudice against minority groups often becomes stronger. People want someone to blame their troubles on. Since the price of goods usually goes up during wartime, and many Jews were merchants or traders, people began to accuse them of raising prices to make money from the war. All businessmen did this in wartime, but the ones people talked about were the Jewish merchants.

Two towns in Georgia voted to order the Jews out. The *Richmond Examiner,* a Virginia newspaper, had so many articles attacking the Jews that a Jewish colonel, Adolphus Adler, challenged the editor to a duel.

Attacks also appeared in northern newspapers. Members of the "Know-Nothing" party, which had been formed mainly to work against Catholics, attacked all immigrants and all minorities.

General Ulysses S. Grant, in the second year of the war, took part in an action against Jews. He ordered all Jewish traders to leave the areas under his command:

> The Jews, as a class violating every regulation of trade established by the Treasury Department and also department orders, are hereby expelled from the department within twenty-four hours from the receipt of this order.

The text of the infamous Order No. 11, issued over the name of General Grant, expelling all Jews from his area. Grant later said he was not responsible for the order, which was cancelled by President Lincoln.

This was, of course, a serious thing to say about the Jews in general. A leading Jewish citizen, Cesar Kaskel, went to Washington right away to see President Lincoln. The very next day, a message went out to General Grant:

> A paper purporting to be General Orders No. 11, issued by you December 17, has been presented here. By its terms, it throws out all Jews from your department. If such an order has been sent out, it will immediately be revoked.

Moses'

Flying

Ambulance.

The surgeon-general of the North was Jonathan Phineas Horwitz. In the Union armies there were many Jewish officers, including several brigadier generals. One was Philip Joachimsen, who had helped convict slavetraders when he was United States Attorney in New York. Edward Solomon was another general. He led an Illinois regiment in which there were over one hundred Jews, and later became Governor of the territory of Washington

There were companies with many Jews in them from Syracuse and Chicago. From Pennsylvania came Cameron's Dragoons, headed by Colonel Max Friedman.

There are records of many deaths of Jews, both on the battlefield and in prison camps. Seven Congressional Medals of Honor were awarded to Jews in the Union Army.

Dr. Israel Moses was a Colonel in the Union Army during the Civil War. He developed a "flying ambulance" which saved the lives of many Union soldiers.

Michael M. Allen of Philadelphia served as unofficial chaplain of "Cameron's Dragoons," a Pennsylvania Cavalry Regiment in which were many Jews, headed by Colonel Max Friedman.

Abraham Lincoln's Relations With Jews

Lincoln acted quickly, but the hurt remained. It made it seem as if Jews were not to be trusted. Jews held many meetings of protest and articles were written for the papers to answer the false accusations that were being made. General Grant made a public apology later.

This was not the only time that the Jews had to ask President Lincoln to step in. Early in the war, Congress had passed a law that would allow troops to have a chaplain. It said that each chaplain "must be a regular ordained minister of some Christian group." Michael Allen, a Jew and chaplain of Cameron's Dragoons, had

to resign. Arnold Fischel of New York went to Washington for the Jewish Board of Delegates to take the matter up with the government.

Fischel appealed to both houses of Congress, saying that the law was not fair. It was against the Constitution, he reminded them, "to require a religious test as a qualification for an officer under the United States." He was able to see Lincoln himself who promised, "I shall try to have a new law broad enough to cover what is desired by you in behalf of the Israelites." The new law said that chaplains had to be ministers "of some religious denomination.*" This permitted rabbis to serve.

Lincoln knew many Jews. Abraham Kohn, city clerk of Chicago, was thanked by Lincoln for presenting him with a painting of the flag on which were printed verses from the biblical book of

The Rev. Arnold Fischel of New York. His petition to the President and Senate brought about a change in the law that military chaplains had to be members of "some Christian denomination."

Joshua: "Be strong and of good courage; be not affrighted, neither be thou dismayed; for the Lord thy God is with thee whithersoever thou goest."

An old friend of President Lincoln, who had served with him in the Illinois legislature, was Abraham Jonas of Quincy. Four sons of Jonas, however, fought for the Confederacy. One was captured by Union forces. The President sadly wrote an order in his own hand:

Allow Charles H. Jonas, now a prisoner of war at Johnson's Island, a parole of three weeks to visit his dying father, Abraham Jonas, at Quincy, Illinois.

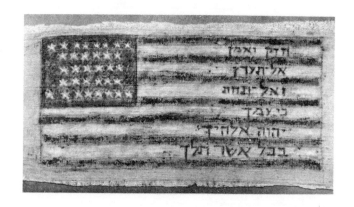

Abraham Kohn, city clerk of Chicago and ardent Lincoln supporter, presented a painting of the American flag to Lincoln at the time of his inauguration, bearing the Hebrew words from the book of Joshua: "Be strong and of good courage; be not afraid nor dismayed; for the Lord your God is with you wherever you go."

The end of the war had hardly been celebrated when the terrible news of the assassination of President Lincoln rocked the country. Along with the rest of the people, the Jews mourned his death. They appreciated and loved him as a just and kindly president.

To many people of every race and creed, Lincoln, who had freed the slaves, remained the greatest of heroes. He became a symbol of freedom to those seeking freedom all over the world.

Charles H. Jonas, a friend of Abraham Lincoln. The President issued the famous "furlough order" allowing Jonas's son, a Confederate soldier and prisoner of war, to visit his dying father.

A definition of democracy in Abraham Lincoln's own handwriting.

CHAPTER X

Reform, Conservative, Orthodox

"Each congregation pursues its own way, has its own customs and mode of worship. One Jew is a stranger in the synagogue of another."

Isaac Mayer Wise observed this when he arrived in the United States at the age of twenty-seven from his homeland of Bohemia, now a part of Czechoslovakia. Orthodox congregations differed among themselves. One synagogue followed the Portuguese or Sephardi ritual, another the German, and still another the Polish way of conducting the service. There were different ways of pronouncing the Hebrew words, different melodies for the prayers, and different customs of carrying on the service.

There were also three Reform temples, Beth Elohim in Charleston, Har Sinai in Baltimore, and Emanu-El in New York, which had shortened their services, introduced the organ, and used German and English besides Hebrew. This made for even more striking differences in the practice of Judaism.

The minhag (which means "custom" or "observance") or ritual of each congregation was different. What Isaac Mayer Wise sought was one "minhag America," one "American way" of Jewish religious life.

Wise had been interested, for some years, in the German Reform movement. He brought the idea of Reform Judaism to his own congregation in Albany, arranging for a choir to sing English hymns, allowing families to sit together instead of separating men and women, as was done in the traditional synagogue, and trying to make the service more modern and meaningful to the members of the congregation, most of whom came from Germany.

Isaac Mayer Wise (1818-1900), American Reform rabbi, founder of the Union of American Hebrew Congregations, the Hebrew Union College, and the Central Conference of American Rabbis. He was also a civic leader, editor, writer and publisher.

Title page of the first Reform prayer-book to appear in America. It was prepared by Rabbis Kalish, Wise and Rothenheim, and was issued in English, German and Hebrew.

He started a day school which taught English, German, and Jewish subjects to the children of the congregation. Instead of the Bar Mitzvah ceremony, a Confirmation service for girls as well as for boys was planned.

Some of his members did not want these changes. Those who liked his ideas started a new congregation, where Rabbi Wise could carry out all his reforms. In the new Temple, the rabbi changed the prayers that spoke of the return to Zion and the rebuilding of the Temple in Jerusalem. For him, America was the Promised Land. The Jews were a religious group, he felt, not a people with hopes for a nation of their own.

Ten years after his arrival in America, Rabbi Wise went to Cincinnati, to be the rabbi of Congregation B'nai Yeshurun. By this time, his name and his ideas were known all over the country. Isaac Leeser gave him space to express his ideas in the *Occident*. With his colleague Max Lilienthal, Rabbi Wise edited his own magazines, *The Israelite* and *Die Deborah*. In

Temple Emanuel of New York as it appeared in 1868, at the corner of Fifth Avenue and Forty-Third Street. It is now located at Fifth Avenue and Sixty-Fifth Street.

The first issue of *Die Deborah*, a German-language supplement to *The Israelite*, both published by Isaac Mayer Wise, so as to reach both English and German-speaking Jews in America.

them he expressed his love for Jewish tradition and the Hebrew language. He wrote articles calling for all Jews in America to unite and strengthen their faith.

Reform rabbis of America, like those in the German states, felt that Jews no longer had to keep the many ritual laws of the Bible and Talmud. They did not think that Jewish law should tell people what to eat, how to prepare their food, or how to rest on Shabbat. The important Jewish teachings had to do with ideas of justice and brotherhood.

There were rabbis in the east who held radical Reform beliefs, like David Einhorn and Samuel Hirsch. These men were much more extreme than Wise. For example, they held their Sabbath services on Sunday, when most Americans went to prayer services. Rabbi Wise, however, believing that the Ten Commandments had been given by God on Mount Sinai, and could not be changed, insisted that the Sabbath must be kept on the seventh day, as it is written.

Isaac Mayer Wise joined with Isaac Leeser to call a meeting of rabbis in Cleveland. Both hoped for a minhag America, for one central religious group to which all American Jews could belong. Rabbi Wise did not believe that Jews in modern America should be required to keep the laws of the Talmud, but he knew that Leeser and other traditional Jews did so believe. He said at this meeting, because unity was so important to him, that all should agree on the importance of the Talmud in Jewish life.

The radical Reform rabbis could not agree to this. They had spoken out against keeping traditional laws of kashrut,* Shabbat,* the wearing of kipah* and talit,* circumcision, conversion, and many of the laws of marriage and divorce. They had dropped the second day of holidays, which had been adopted outside the land of Israel after the Exile. More important than the obeying of laws was their belief that Jews were a religious group with a mission to spread light among the nations. They felt that Talmudic law was not necessary for the making of a better world, and that it therefore was not holy or binding.

Jews who considered all of Jewish tradition holy, and who wished to keep not only the ritual and ethical laws, but also the national hopes of the Jewish people, could not join in action with the Reform group. The Cleveland meeting failed, but Rabbi Wise kept working for a union. In 1873 he finally gathered representatives of many non-orthodox congregations to form the Union of American Hebrew Congregations.

A very early photograph of the Hebrew Union College building in Cincinnati.

A very early photograph of the Jewish Theological Seminary of America, in New York.

Two years later, in 1875, he helped found the first successful rabbinical seminary in America, the Hebrew Union College. Isaac Mayer Wise was president of the College, and became a professor at the school as well. Now there would be English-speaking rabbis and leaders for American Jewry.

The Development Of Conservative Judaism

In spite of his great desire for unity, Rabbi Wise's school or type of Judaism could not be supported and adopted by all Jews. Traditional and observing Jews were heartened by Wise's success in starting a seminary, but they wanted one that would teach their kind of Judaism. In 1886, the rabbis and scholars who wanted a rabbinical school that would teach modern and ethical ideas while at the same time conserving (or holding on to) Jewish tradition, founded the Jewish Theological Seminary of America in New York. Among them were Sabato Morais,

an Italian Jew who had lived and studied in England and who became president of the Seminary; Alexander Kohut, who had been a liberal member of the Hungarian parliament; Benjamin Szold of Baltimore, and Marcus Jastrow of Philadelphia.

The seminary became the school of the Conservative movement. Conservative Jews believe with Reform that Judaism has always grown and changed through the ages, and that it is still changing. Conservative Judaism differs, however, in stressing that Jewish traditions and customs must be respected, that change must be gradual, and that the Jews are a people who should continue to keep the age-old Jewish hope for renewed life and return to Zion.

Sabato Morais (1823-1897), rabbi at Mikveh Israel, traditional Jew, scholar and abolitionist. He was a founder of the Conservative movement, and president of the Jewish Theological Seminary from its founding in 1886 until his death.

Many Jews Remained Orthodox

Most Jews who came to America as immigrants toward the end of the Nineteenth Century did not know the words Reform and Conservative. They knew only the traditional way of life as it had been followed in the towns they came from. If they wished to set up a synagogue, they wanted it to be like the

Rabbi Jacob Joseph, scholar brought from Europe by leading Orthodox Jewish congregations of New York in an effort to unite the community.

rituals, they are both part of the Orthodox wing of Judaism. In 1898, Hazzan Henry Pereira Mendes, who led the Spanish and Portuguese congregation, Shearith Israel, helped to establish the Union of Orthodox Jewish Congregations of the United States and Canada.

The many small Orthodox congregations were not eager to join together. Each congregation had its own traditions and kept its synagogue going the way its members liked it. They usually chose rabbis who were trained in Europe. Many, though they were scholars of the Talmud, knew little of America, and spoke Yiddish, not English. They often had little influence with younger, American-born members.

איינע גראסע

מאססענפערזאמלונג

פאן אנטי קאראבקע (טאקסע)

ווירד שטאטטפינדען אם זאננטאג דען 13טען יאנואר 1889 אום 3 אוהר נאך מיטטאג

אין פהעניקס האלל 73 לודלאוו סטריט,

ברידער!

אזוי וויא אייך איז בעקאנט דאס ר׳ יעקב דער מגיד פן ווילנא מאכט שוין צו פיעל ביזנעס רשם שמים און סאקט אויס בײא אונז דען לעטצטען בענעט אונטער דער מאסקע פן רעליגיאן. עף מאכט קא־ ראבקעס פן פלײש, מצה, און ווין; סיינס און פלאמבעס און בעריינבט דאס ארמע פאלק אים נאמען דער רעליגיאן און ער זעלבסט האלט ניט פן דת משה, רען ער האט נים גיעוואלט ניעהן צו דיה.

אלזא ברידער קומט צו דיעס מאסטענמיטונג פאר אייער אײגענע אינטערעסע זיך צו בעראטהען.

דאס קאמיטע.

GRAND MASS MEETING

— OF THE —

ANTI-TAXES & RELIGION CONTRIBUTION

OF THE IMPORTED RABBI,

Will take place on Sunday, January 13th '89 3 P. M.

At Phoenix Hall 73 Ludlow St.,

Ein Grosser Massnversammlung gegen die Religion-Steuer fon den Importirten Magid, am Sonntag den 13, Januar um 3 Uhr n. M. In Phoenix Hall 73 Ludlow St. Stattfinden wird.

Notice of a mass meeting protesting against Chief Rabbi Jacob Joseph of New York. Many objected to paying any kind of tax in order to support the rabbi.

Ashkenazi one they remembered in Eastern Europe.

Ashkenazi Jews, in colonial times, joined the Sephardi synagogues that the first settlers had started. By the time of the Revolution, there were more Ashkenazim than Sephardim in the Sephardic synagogues. In the Nineteenth Century there were enough Ashkenazi Jews from Europe to set up their own type of synagogue, first in Philadelphia and then in New York. In 1852, immigrants from Russia and Poland started a *shul** in New York. This was the first of hundreds of shuls to be founded by East European Jews, when they arrived in greater numbers during the next seventy years.

Although Ashkenazi and Sephardi synagogues follow somewhat different

Fifteen of the East European Orthodox synagogues in New York tried to unite their community by bringing a great scholar from Europe to be their Chief Rabbi. They hoped that he would gain the respect of all, and would be able to see that Jewish law was observed and that proper standards of kashrut were kept. They invited Rabbi Jacob Joseph of Vilna. The pious scholar came unwillingly, and was greatly disappointed. He was not able to unite the Orthodox community of New York.

Traditional Jews, however, continued to found and support Orthodox synagogues, and faithfully to observe the traditions and rituals of the past.

In the free atmosphere of America, where a man can choose his own way of life, a great number of different religious sects grew up among Christians. The Jews have not divided into sects in that sense. Although they have divided into Orthodox, Conservative, and Reform branches, they do not regard themselves as belonging to different religions. And they certainly feel that they are of the same people. When it comes to taking action to help Jews in need, Jews of all branches work together. But when it comes to synagogue customs and daily rituals, they prefer to choose their own way.

Despite the lack of unity, the fears of both Isaac Leeser and Isaac Mayer Wise that the whole community might disappear, have not come true. American Jews of all three groups are loyal to their faith and people.

CHAPTER XI

Mother Of Exiles

The Statue of Liberty stands in New York Harbor. Those who visit it can climb up to the crown and can see the torch of hope uplifted in the hand of this "mighty woman." Below, on the wall, is a plaque on which is engraved a poem. The name of this figure, says the poem, is "Mother of Exiles." Its last lines state:

Give me your tired, your poor,
Your huddled masses yearning to
   breathe free,
The wretched refuse of your teeming
   shore,
Send these, the homeless, tempest-
   tossed to me.
I lift my lamp beside the golden door!

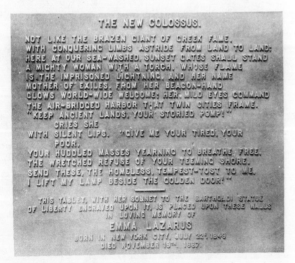

A tablet in the Statue of Liberty with Emma Lazarus's sonnet "The New Colossus".

The Statue of Liberty, symbol of America's welcome to the "masses, yearning to breathe free," of Europe.

These words, written by the Jewish poet Emma Lazarus in 1883, tell in a few words what America seemed to say at that time to the people of Europe!

Immigration After the Civil War

Indeed, in the United States after the Civil War, there was room for millions of newcomers. It was a large country that reached from coast to coast. Railroads crossed the land. New open territories were being settled and, as soon as there were enough people in them, they became states and were added to the United States. Job of all kinds were open in this uncrowded, growing land.

In such a developing society, immigrants were welcomed. All over Europe, people who had a hard time making a living looked to America as the land of opportunity. Here, they were needed. Some came to spend a few years working for high wages, planning to go back later to their families in Poland or Greece or Italy. Most, however, stayed on. After working hard and saving money for some years, they were able to bring brothers and sisters, parents and wives, to join them.

Between 1870 and 1920, thirty million immigrants came to the United States. Of these, two and a half million were Jews.

IMMIGRATION BY PERIODS: 1840–1953

year	Jewish immigrants	total immigrants
1840–1870	150,000	6,700,000
1871–1890	250,000	8,000,000
1891–1925	2,200,000	22,000,000
1926–1953	400,000	3,000,000

The lure of freedom and high wages drew an ever-increasing stream of immigrants to America from Europe. This woodcut shows Britain trying to hold back workers who wish to go to the United States.

Why did so many Jews come? Like other immigrants, they wanted to live in a land whose doctrine was "that all men are created equal." They wanted to be able to send their children to school. They did not want to be drafted to serve in wars of kings and czars.

This drawing illustrates "eager immigrants," ten million of whom entered the United States between 1860 and 1890.

The Jews came to America for the same reasons that others did, and for other, more serious reasons as well. They wanted to live in a place where there would not be special laws against them because of their religion. They wanted, as Emma Lazarus wrote, "Freedom to love the law that Moses brought, To sing the songs of David. . . . Freedom to dig the common earth, to drink the universal* air." None of these freedoms were truly theirs in Eastern Europe.

Emma Lazarus (1849-1887), Jewish poet of New York, who was aroused by the plight of the Russian Jews to study her people's history and language and to write about their life and faith.

Emma Lazarus

Emma Lazarus was born in the United States, and like many native Americans, grew up without thinking much about her fellow Jews across the sea. She lived in New York with her well-to-do family, studied, and read books, and wrote poetry. She went, sometimes, to Sabbath or Holiday services at the Shearith Israel congregation to which her parents belonged.

Emma Lazarus knew that far away there were Jews who lived in Russia and Poland, Hungary, Rumania, and Lithuania. She knew they were mostly rather poor, that they loved study and prayer and the celebration of Jewish holidays, that they were old-fashioned and different from herself.

Her main interest was in writing. She read the works of American poets like Emerson, and English poets like Byron. She wrote poems with titles like "Fantasies," "Spring Star," "Autumn Sadness." She liked to write about Greek gods and old stories of the ancient world.

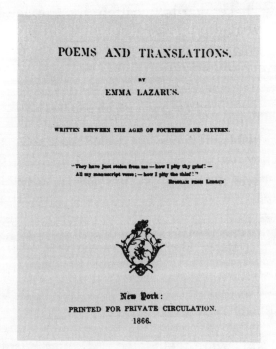

Title page of a book by Emma Lazarus.

In 1881, her interests began to change. Russia became part of her thoughts. It was well known that there were groups who wanted to overthrow the czar. Most of the people of Russia were poor and without civil rights. In that year, someone threw a bomb at the carriage of Czar Alexander II, killing him. Some thought the revolution would now begin. But the next czar acted fast. Alexander III arrested all suspected

Caricature by Daumier showing Czar Nicholas I extracting money from his Jewish subjects.

radicals and took away the freedoms that had been granted by his father.

The new czar had to find ways of turning the anger of the people away from the rulers. All sorts of propaganda was spread, to make the peasants feel that the czar was their "father" and that they must hate his enemies. Much of the propaganda was against the Jews, who were pictured as the enemies of Christianity and its way of life. By making them angry against Jews they had no time to think of who was really oppressing them.

Gangs of Russians attacked and killed Jewish men, women and children, and burned the homes and stores of Jews in a dozen different cities. The Russian police did nothing to help the victims or to arrest the hoodlums. The fact was that many of the gangs had been organized by government agents. Newspaper articles and speeches in churches kept telling the people of Russia that the Jews were to blame for all their troubles.

News of the pogroms* was printed in newspapers throughout the world. Emma Lazarus read of the terrible events, and was suddenly impressed with the fact that although these were her people, she knew so little about them!

The Bishop of Ripon at a meeting at the London Guildhall in 1890, leading a protest against the persecution of the Jews of Russia.

In Russia, laws were passed, called the May Laws of 1882, ordering the Jews to crowd into ghetto districts even smaller than those they were living in. They were no longer allowed to live in villages or in many of the areas where they had made their homes. The new laws cut down the kinds of jobs and types of work that Jews would be permitted to do. They would not be allowed to keep their stores open on Sundays, even though they were already closed on Saturdays. A school quota was set up allowing only a tiny number of Jews to enter high schools or universities. Those who had been given special permission to live in large cities were now told to leave them.

It became almost impossible for Jews to support themselves, and official antisemitism was becoming stronger year by

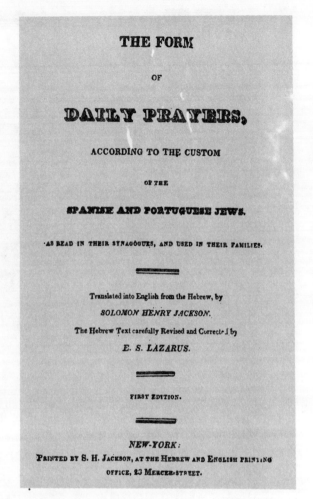

THE FORM

OF

DAILY PRAYERS,

ACCORDING TO THE CUSTOM

OF THE

SPANISH AND PORTUGUESE JEWS.

AS READ IN THEIR SYNAGOGUES, AND USED IN THEIR FAMILIES.

Translated into English from the Hebrew, by
SOLOMON HENRY JACKSON.

The Hebrew Text carefully Revised and Corrected by
E. S. LAZARUS.

FIRST EDITION.

NEW-YORK:
PRINTED BY S. H. JACKSON, AT THE HEBREW AND ENGLISH PRINTING
OFFICE, 23 MERCER-STREET.

This edition of the prayer book was prepared by E.S. Lazarus, grandfather of Emma Lazarus, in 1826.

year. A flood-tide of Jews began to leave Russia and the part of Poland ruled by the czars.

Emma Lazarus was one of the many American Jews who went to the aid of the Jewish immigrants when they landed here. The shock of the pogroms had led her to write with sympathy of her people's plight:

> A million burning rooftrees light
> The world-wide path of Israel's
> flight.

She had begun to study about her people and their ideals. She learned Hebrew and read Jewish history. She began to appreciate the great ideals that her people had kept alive. She learned also of the hope many Jews had for a return to the land of Israel. She read of the Russian Jews who were known as the "Lovers of Zion," who in the 1870s and 1880s took the dangerous journey to Palestine, which was then ruled by an unfriendly Turkish government. She wrote of the Jews who chose to go to the ancient promised land, the land of Israel, and of those who came to the West:

> In two divided streams the exiles
> part,
> One rolling homeward to its ancient
> source,
> One rushing sunward with fresh
> will, new heart.

Most Jews who left Russia turned toward the West. Some settled in France, Germany, or England. Some went to other continents, to South Africa, to Canada, Argentina, even to New Zealand and Australia. All these were, at the time, willing to let immigrants in because they needed workers.

The largest number, however, came to the United States. The number increased year after year. They came not only from Russia itself, but from the Polish province of Galicia, from Rumania, and from all of Eastern Europe.

Most of the immigrants had little money and little knowledge of the outside world. Often the only language they spoke was Yiddish. Fellow Jews tried to help them on their journey, in every land they traveled through.

In the United States, Jews who were well-to-do and respected citizens gave money and time to help the newcomers.

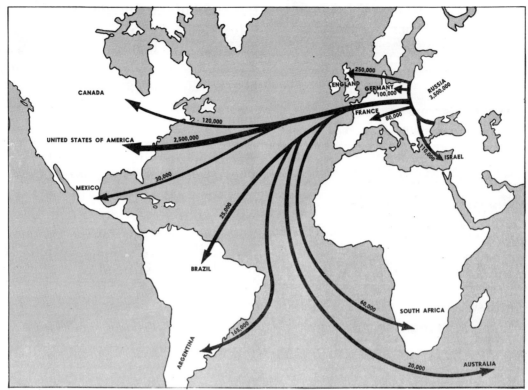

This map shows where Jews went from Eastern Europe between the years 1881 and 1932. The vast majority came to the United States.

They might feel embarrassed that their new-found "cousins" were not educated gentlemen and ladies, but poorly-dressed wanderers who did not know the English language or modern ways of life. But it is to the credit of the so-called "German" Jews, those whose families had lived in America since the early part of the century, that they wanted to help their brethren.

Emma Lazarus, the gentle Sephardic Jew, saw nobility even in the bent and emaciated immigrant. She spoke of them in the words of the prophet Ezekiel:

What, can these dead bones live,
    whose sap is dried
By twenty scorching centuries of
    wrong?

She praised the Jew of Eastern Europe for his loyalty to learning all through the centuries:

High above flood and fire ye held the
    scroll,
Out of the depths ye published still
    the Word.

When she was a young poet, Emma had been praised by the leading writer of America, Ralph Waldo Emerson. She had been overjoyed to have American poets interested in her writings. One of them had told her her poems were good, but that he thought she would be a greater writer if she used more "Hebrew" ideas. He was right. Her awakened interest in her tradition, aroused by her people's suffering, gave her poems fire and feeling. She learned Hebrew well enough to translate the work of Hebrew poets. She chose for her heroes Bar Kochba and the Maccabees, and even the commentator Rashi, and wrote of brave Jewish martyrs dying for their faith instead of Greek gods pining for love.

107

She longed for all Jews to feel the love and pride she felt for her people. She wanted all to join with the newcomers in their devotion to Torah and their love of Zion:

Oh for Jerusalem's trumpet now
To blow a blast of shattering
    power,
To wake the sleepers high and low,
    And rouse them to the urgent hour!
No hand for vengeance but to save,
A million naked swords should
    wave.

O deem not dead that martial fire,
    Say not the mystic flame is spent!
With Moses' law and David's lyre,
    Your ancient strength remains un-
    bent.
Let but an Ezra rise anew.
To lift the Banner of the Jew!

Henrietta Szold

In the "urgent hour" another young American woman, very much affected by

Henrietta Szold (1860-1945), scholar, humanitarian and Zionist leader. After a distinguished career as educator and editor, she founded Hadassah, and settled in Jerusalem, where she supervised Hadassah's medical and social services, and headed Youth Aliyah.

the flight of the Russian Jews, came to the fore. Henrietta Szold was the brilliant daughter of Rabbi Benjamin Szold of Baltimore. To this port city, also, came many of the immigrants.

By the age of seventeen, Henrietta Szold was already a high school teacher! She was also a writer for Anglo-Jewish magazines, a religious-school teacher and a research assistant to her father.

She was twenty-one in 1881, the year when immigrants began coming in large numbers. Her father welcomed and helped the newcomers. Henrietta decided that the greatest need of the immigrants was for education in English. Single-

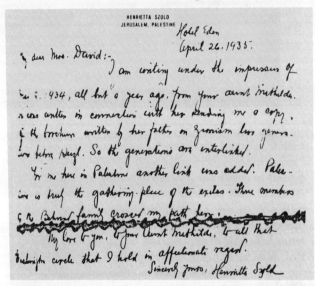

Excerpts from a letter of Henrietta Szold, telling that "Palestine is truly the gathering place of the exiles." Miss Szold died before the birth of the State of Israel.

handed at first, she set up evening schools where adults could come after their day's work. As the organizer and main teacher, she enabled older people to learn to read and write English. She also taught American history and civics so that they would be able to pass the test to become citizens.

In her years of work with evening schools, Henrietta Szold helped over

Caricature of Irishman reading about New York. The potato famine in Ireland during the late 1840s caused over a million Irishmen to migrate to America.

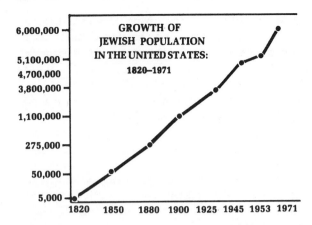

GROWTH OF JEWISH POPULATION IN THE UNITED STATES: 1820–1971

The growth of the Jewish population in the United States from 1820 until recent times.

5000 immigrants to take their place in the life of this country. She was able to give up the work when the city of Baltimore established its own evening schools for adults. Her example was followed by other cities as well.

In the year 1881 there were about 250,000 Jews in the United States. The number grew ten times, to 2,500,000, in the next thirty years. Most of the Jews of America today are descendants of the East European Jews who started coming in large numbers after the pogroms of 1881 and the May Laws of 1882.

Are you, perhaps, one of them?

America, Land of Immigrants

From the beginning, most of the settlers in the American colonies were from England and the British Isles. Very early, of course, there were also Dutch, French, Spanish, and Scandinavian settlers, and pioneers from other countries as well. Many of those who went to Canada were French; and Frenchmen also settled the Louisiana area. Spanish explorers, traders and missionaries opened up California and areas near to Mexico.

Three million Africans were brought to the Colonies as slaves from 1619 on. The largest number went to plantations in the South. There were blacks, however, from earliest times in every part of the country, including free men who settled in the north or traveled westward.

There were many immigrants before the Civil War from Ireland, because of the famine there in the 1840s. Scandinavians and Germans also came in large numbers.

Later, when wars and revolutions upset lives in Europe, and farms became poorer and towns became crowded, America seemed more than ever the land of promise. Those "yearning to breathe free" in Italy and Greece, and other lands near the Mediterranean Sea, and in the countries of Eastern Europe (Hungary, Rumania, Poland, Russia) came in great numbers to America.

Thirty million immigrants came in the fifty years following 1870. Of these, two and a half million were Jews.

Most of the non-Jewish settlers in America were from England and the British Isles, and this decided what the language of the country would be. However, many of those who went to Canada were French, and Frenchmen also settled in the Louisiana area. So French was spoken in those places. Wherever Spanish explorers went, followed by missionaries and settlers and traders, there Spanish was spoken.

The three million Africans who were brought here as slaves lost the native tongues they had spoken in their own lands. They came to speak the language of their masters, English.

Later, when Germans came, and large numbers from Italy, Greece, and countries of Eastern Europe, one could hear all of their languages in the streets of America. The Jews among them added the Yiddish tongue. As with the others, however, the children of the Jewish immigrants began to use English as their native tongue, and Yiddish, like Greek, Hungarian, Rumanian and other languages of the immigrants began to be heard less and less.

All Jews Are Responsible For One Another

Jews have lived in Poland and Russia for over a thousand years. Jews left the Germanic states of western Europe at times of persecution, and went eastward. The largest number went to Poland, for during the Middle Ages, they were invited by Polish kings to come to their land.

Most of the Jews from western Europe spoke a dialect of German; they continued to speak this language in the homes and communities they came to. With much Hebrew added, and also some words of Russian or Polish adopted from their neighbors, the language developed into a thoroughly Jewish tongue called Yiddish. Besides Hebrew, it is the greatest of the languages of the Jewish people.

It was spoken by about twelve million people at the beginning of this century, and many Yiddish writers left beautiful pictures of the life of the people in the Jewish *shtetl.* *

In Poland, Lithuania and Russia, there were periods of peace and Jews were able to build great communities where the study of Torah reached its height. Life in the Jewish community was lived according to Jewish law. There was charity and helpfulness for those in need. But life was also disturbed from time to time by pogroms, expulsions, and persecutions. After 1881, great numbers began to leave Eastern Europe.

Jews formed all kinds of organizations, and Jewish philanthropists, wealthy men who believed in the *mitzvah* * of *tzedakah,* * (the commandment to help others) gave of their wealth to aid the Jewish immigrants in every land. Maurice de Hirsch was allowed to open offices in Russia. His aim was to have Jews trained to become farmers and technical workers,

Model of a wooden synagogue in Poland, in the 1600s, the type that was built by an entire community.

110

and to encourage them to settle in Argentina. Some followed his plan, but so many more went to New York that he set up his main offices there.

Polish Jews asking advice about emigrating to the United States, at the information desk of the Hebrew Immigrant Aid Society in Warsaw.

Baron Maurice de Hirsch (1831-1896), banker and railroad magnate of Paris, who gave over 100 million dollars in philanthropy. He fostered agriculture, crafts and education in the Jewish communities of the world, and helped new settlers in America and Argentina.

In America other helpful organizations sprang up, among them the Hebrew Immigrant Aid Society, known as HIAS, and the National Council of Jewish Women. There were also *landsmanshaft-en*,* societies of people who came from the same town or area in the old country, who would help each other in every way.

Mauricia, Jewish farm colony in Argentina founded by the Jewish Colonization Association of Baron de Hirsch for East European Jews who wished to settle there.

111

CHAPTER XII

In The Golden Land

A boy and a girl stood with their mother on the deck of a steamship entering New York Harbor.

The woman wore a long skirt and several sweaters, and had a shawl wrapped around her head. The children were dressed in their good clothes, the boy in knickers and jacket and the girl in an embroidered wool dress. Both wore boots. They had come from a town where roads were snow-filled in winter and muddy in summer.

"When will we see papa?" asked the boy in Yiddish.

"Soon, Yankel, soon," said the mother.

"How will we recognize him?" asked the girl. "We have not seen him for six years."

"Don't worry," said the mother. "He will know us."

Near the family was a cardboard suitcase tied with rope. All around them stood other little groups of people, with their belongings in battered valises or cloth-wrapped bundles at their sides.

Immigrant Jews on the deck of the steamship bringing them to America hail the Statue of Liberty in New York harbor as the symbol of their new life in the free country.

112

Newly arrived Jewish exiles from Russia in the 1880s, leaving Castle Garden for the immigrants' housing on Ward's Island.

Coming to America

The passengers had made a long journey together. They had come from different lands. Some told how they had bribed guards and crossed borders at night. They had traveled by coach and by train, and sometimes on foot, to reach the harbor on the western shore of Europe. There they had boarded the ship that would take them across the Atlantic.

For very low fares, they had been allowed to bunk below decks, near the noise of the engines, in the section called "steerage.*" There they found little space and few comforts. Rough seas made many of them sick. Babies cried all night. The family of Yankel, like many others, had

brought their own kosher food. By this time, they were tired and hungry, but they were happy.

"Look at the big tall buildings, Mama!" the little girl called out. "Are we going to live in one of them?"

A woman near them spoke in Polish to her children. "This is New York. We will go to Chicago with Uncle Stanislaus. Chicago is a big city too."

"We go to Minnesota to our cousin's farm," said a traveler from Sweden.

Suddenly a hum of voices was heard, then a cheer. Little children were lifted high to see.

"Look, Yankele, Sorele," the mother said. "The Statue of Liberty. She says, Welcome to the Golden Land."

113

A street in the "ghetto" in New York City.

Jewish tradition was observed even amidst the poverty of the ghetto. This poor Jew is preparing for the Sabbath in his cellar home.

The family, like others, had to stop first at Ellis Island. Father was waiting for them to help them to talk to the United States immigration officers. One even spoke to them in Yiddish. Some travelers who were ill or alone, and had no jobs waiting for them, were told to wait. Friends came forward to help them, from HIAS, the Hebrew Immigrant Aid Society, or some other group. Otherwise they might have been sent back to Europe.

In New York, the family of Yankel and Sarah lived in an apartment in a tenement house. It was in a poor crowded neighborhood where many immigrant Jews lived. People called the area a "ghetto."

The ghetto in Europe was a place where Jews were forced to live. There was often a wall around it, and nobody was allowed to go in or out without permission. The "ghettos" of America, on the Lower East Side of New York or the West Side of Chicago, were not really the same. There were no walls, and the people could go when and where they wished. They chose to live there themselves, usually because they could not afford to live anywhere else.

Yankel and Sarah thought their father had become rich in the new country. After all, he had sent them money and steamship tickets. They soon realized, however, that there was not much money for luxuries in the new home. They also learned that they would see very little of their father. He went to work early, and often did not come home until after they were asleep. He had to work ten or twelve

A sweatshop on Ludlow Street in New York City. Notice the Hebrew wedding certificate (Ketubah) on the wall.

Inside a clothing factory in 1912.

hours in a factory six days a week, in order to make enough to feed his family.

Many of the Jewish men and women in their neighborhood were clothing workers. The making of suits and coats, shirts and caps, had once been done in people's homes or in small shops. Then, ready-to-wear clothing began to be made with the help of sewing machines in factories. More and more workers were needed as more people bought their clothes in stores.

Factory owners in this growing industry often came to the docks to hire the immigrants as workers. Newcomers were glad to take any work they could get. Owners of companies did not have to pay high wages. If a worker did not like the conditions, he could leave; there were hundreds of others coming in to take his place.

The hot crowded rooms where work was done were called "sweatshops." There was not enough air or light. Workers often became ill with tuberculosis or other diseases. There was also danger of fire in the unsafe buildings. In one famous fire in a shirt factory, 146 workers, most of them Jewish young women, were killed.

The Union Makes Us Strong

The father of Yankel and Sarah used to talk about the union. "We should not have to work sixty hours a week," he

Fellow Workers!

Join in rendering a last sad tribute of sympathy and affection for the victims of the Triangle Fire. THE FUNERAL PROCESSION will take place Wednesday, April 5th, at 1 P. M. Watch the newspapers for the line of march.

צו דער לויה שװעסטער און ברידער!

די לויה פון די היילינע קרבנות פון דעם טרייענגעל פייער װעט זיין סימװאך, דעם 5טען אפריל, 1 אזאר נאכמיטטאג.

קיינער פון אייך זאר ניט פערבלייבען אין די שעפער! שליסט זיך צו אין די רייהען פון די סטריייקענדע! דריקט אויס אייער סימפאטיע און סיטפען בעדויערען אין אייף דעם נדיסקן פערלוסם װאם די ארבייטערװעלט האט געהאט

געבראכט די קנע — סים ציסעתתען הערצער זאלען סיר פיהרען אונזערע פחייירע שפאגרות צו זיער לעצטער רוה.

חאסמם די עייפוגנען דורך װעלכע סיר װעלען לעזען װיסען װאו איהר קענם זיך צוזאמענ טעזען.

צו דער לויה פון די היילינע קרבנות.
סטם שװעסטער און ברידער!

Operai Italiani!

Unitevi compatti a rendere l'ultimo tributo d'affetto alle vittime dell'imane sciagura della Triangle Waist Co. IL CORTEO FUNEBRE avrà luogo mercoledì, 5 Aprile, alle ore 1 P. M. Traverete nei giornali l'ordine della marcia.

A black bordered circular in three languages (English, Yiddish, Italian) calling upon the people of New York to pay their last respects to the victims of the Triangle Fire. 156 people, mostly Jews, were killed in the fire.

would say. "We should be paid more than five dollars for a week's work. If we have the union, all the workers will join together and ask for better conditions."

"If you complain now, the boss will fire you," said his wife. "But if everyone goes on strike together, and nobody will work until things are changed, maybe the boss will listen."

The International Ladies' Garment Workers' Union was started in 1900. Organizers came to the factory where their father worked. Soon many of the workers joined the union, and demanded shorter hours and higher wages. When the union had a demonstration, the children marched with their parents.

Often, a strike had to be called. While the workers were on strike, they received no pay. But the union members held out until they got raises and some of the other things they were asking for.

"Some men came today and told the boss that they were not members of the union and that they would work even when the other workers are on strike," the father told his family. "Now the union will have to insist on a 'closed shop.' That means that only union members can get work at our factory. Then all the workers will be together and will be able to get better conditions."

With the help of the unions, conditions improved for the family. When the workers in men's clothing formed the Amalgamated Clothing Workers' Union, they were able to get the employers to lessen the number of hours they worked each week to 48.

Most people still worked six days a week. Many of the children's neighbors worked on Shabbat. Some of them wept, but they felt they could not support their families unless they did. It was hard for

Samuel Gompers (1850-1924), a British-born Jew who started as a cigar-maker in New York and became founder and president for 38 years of the American Federation of Labor.

many people to keep Jewish law in the new country.

"The Bible and the Talmud have many laws that protect and help the worker and the poor," their father taught them. "We can be proud that some of the great union leaders are Jews. Sidney Hillman and David Dubinsky are helping all workers, no matter what their religion. The real beginner of the labor movement in this country, Samuel Gompers, is also a Jew."

At first there were many struggles between the employers and the unions. The unions, however, later became helpful to the factory owners as well. Improved conditions and healthier workers meant better work. The unions built apartment houses for their members, and opened up banks and insurance departments to make life for the workers' families more secure. Some of them even provided scholarships to college for children of workers. Some unions ran summer resorts and camps for recreation for the families of members.

Sidney Hillman (1887–1946) was president of the Amalgamated Clothing Workers Union. He believed in cooperation between labor and management.

Becoming Americanized

Yankel and Sarah went to public school. They learned English quickly. Yankel was told his name in English was Jacob. After school, almost every day, the boy attended Hebrew school. Both children found many other things to do. They sometimes went to the Educational Alliance, where there were courses and lectures, art, music and theater groups, and clubs of all kinds.

The YMHA (Young Men's Hebrew Association) and other institutions also offered courses in English and vocational training, as well as sports and clubs. In the famous Henry Street Settlement, founded by Lillian Wald, children and their parents could learn how to be healthier and better citizens of the new country.

"It is the uptown Jews who give the money and the teachers for these things," their mother told them. "They may be German Jews, and they may be proud, but they know they are Jews all the same, and they try to help."

Many of the neighbors went to meetings of different Jewish organizations. Some of these had started in Europe. There were Zionist groups for those who were most interested in rebuilding the land of Israel. There were socialist groups who wanted to improve society and fight for workers' rights, like the *Arbeiter Ring*, or Workmen's Circle, which organized Yiddish schools and other cultural activities.

Jews of all ages reading in the Aguilar Free Library, New York, 1895.

The new immigrants were active both with their hands and with their minds. They had to work hard to earn a living. Gradually, conditions became better, and the people earned more and were able to save some money. They moved to better houses, sometimes away from the "ghetto" to newer sections of the cities, like the Bronx or Brooklyn in New York.

ORIGINS OF JEWISH IMMIGRANTS TO THE UNITED STATES: 1940–1953

country	number of Jews
Germany	250,000
England	150,000
France	50,000
Belgium, Holland, Spain, etc.	50,000
Poland, Russia, Rumania, Hungary, etc.	2,400,000
	2,900,000

Table showing the origins of Jewish immigrants to the United States.

The immigrants and workers, both Jews and non-Jews, through their unions helped to make life better for people. The government passed laws to make working conditions safe and to improve living standards.

Things became better for Yankel and Sarah and their parents. America became more nearly the "Golden Land" they had expected.

Jewish Farmers in America

Most Jewish immigrants settled in the larger cities. About three-quarters of them stayed in New York. Only about 100,000 in all became farmers, but this was an interesting development.

In the lands of Europe, few Jews had been farmers. Their ancestors in Bible times had been shepherds and farmers in ancient Palestine. Not allowed to buy or own land in Europe, they became city folk. The typical Jew lived in a shtetl or small town. European Jews, for the most part, were urban, or city people.

There were young Jews of Eastern Europe, however, who thought the time had come for Jews to return to the soil. *Am Olam* (Eternal People) was the Hebrew name of a movement which tried to establish farm colonies for Jews in America. Some Jews tried to start *kibbutzim** in America, patterned after those in Palestine, where everyone worked together and shared equally. In Louisiana, in Oregon, in South Dakota, Jews started farm colonies, most of which failed because of flood, insects, and other misfortunes.

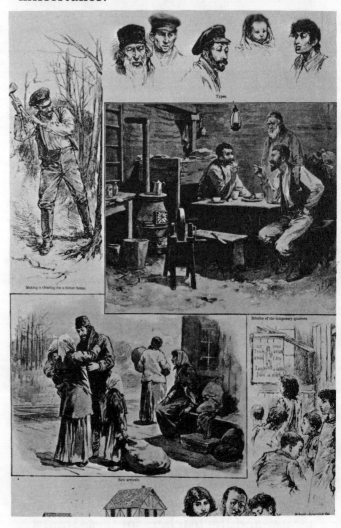

Scenes from the Jewish farm colony at Woodbine, New Jersey, supported by Baron de Hirsch's philanthropy.

Farmers' Synagogue in Toms River, New Jersey. The bulletin board lists the Jewish men and women who served in the Armed Forces in World War II.

An organization of Baron de Hirsch, the HIAS and other groups tried to help Jewish farmers. There was special aid for Jews who landed at Galveston, Texas, to settle in the West rather than in the crowded cities of the East.

Agricultural schools were founded at Woodbine, New Jersey, and in Doyleston, Pennsylvania. The greatest number of successful Jewish farms developed in Carmel and the Vineland and the Lakewood areas of New Jersey.

The great majority of Jewish immigrants, however, settled in cities. By the end of the period of the great immigration, there were two million Jews in New York. There were 200,000 in Chicago and Philadelphia, and over 100,000 in Boston. There were two dozen communities of 20,000 or more Jews scattered throughout the United States and Canada.

A farmhouse of a Jewish settler in the Lasker Colony, Kansas, 1885. The farmhouse was constructed of sod.

CHAPTER XIII

People Of The Book

What is the best thing to do in life?
Yankele will learn Torah.

These are words of a lullaby that Yankel's mother sang to him when he was a baby. From the beginning, the Jewish child was taught that education was the most important lifetime job for the Jew.

In the shtetl of Eastern Europe, most Jews could read and write at a time when most of the people around them could not even sign their own names. The boys studied in *cheder** every day, and many went on to learn Talmud in yeshivot. Grown-ups did not stop studying. Poor tradespeople and hard-working tailors

Young Yeshiva students in Europe.

often belonged to a study group that met daily or on Shabbat, to learn Talmud or read the book of Psalms.

A woman in the Old Country might keep the store as well as care for home and children, so that her husband could spend time with the holy books. In the shtetl, the man who was learned in Talmud got the most respect.

It was hard to keep up the tradition of Torah in the new land. Still, many engaged in study, organized little shuls like those in the shtetl, and did their best to see that their sons learned to pray as they did. Some Jewish boys in America went to intensive schools like the European cheder, sometimes for as much as sixteen hours a week, after school and on Sunday. In many cities, Jews set up a community Talmud Torah, an afternoon school which met three or four times a week.

Many Jewish children studied in Sunday schools. Like most of the non-Jewish children of America, they had about two hours a week of religious training. This gave them a glimpse of Jewish culture, but there was not enough time to learn Hebrew or to appreciate much of the 3500 years of Jewish tradition.

Some American boys went to Heder, studying Torah in the way it had been studied in Europe, for many hours each week.

With all the problems of hard work, poverty, and living in a strange land, many parents did not succeed in giving their children a Jewish education. In America there was no strong Jewish community to which everyone belonged and in which every child lived according to the tradition, as there had been in the shtetl. Many children grew up knowing little of what it meant to be a Jew. Some even thought being a good Jew was an old-fashioned or foreign thing, which had been all right for their parents but was not for them.

Rabbis and teachers and other Jewish leaders tried to make Jewish education better and to see that all children had a chance to learn in a pleasant school. A Jewish Education Committee was set up in New York, and Hebrew High Schools were organized. Other cities set up bureaus of Jewish education and high schools, and more attention was given to the Jewish schools so as to make them more attractive than the old time cheder. As synagogues became larger, they started Hebrew, Sunday, and afternoon schools for the children of their members.

Many teachers in the religious schools came from Eastern Europe, where they had learned Hebrew and Talmud. There was need for teacher-training in America. The Jewish Theological Seminary started its Teachers Institute and College of Jewish Studies, open to women as well as men. Orthodox Jews established Yeshiva College, where students could learn general as well as Jewish subjects. There were also the Herzliah School in New York, and other Hebrew colleges in big cities like Boston, Baltimore, Philadelphia and Chicago.

Students studying Talmud at Yeshiva University.

121

Girls as well as boys were now able to consider becoming Hebrew teachers when they grew up, something that had not been heard of in Europe. In the synagogue schools, many of the teachers were women.

The science department in the Jewish Manual Training School in Chicago in 1892. Education was not compulsory for older children, but charitable groups set up schools and training centers such as this.

The Public School: Doorway to a New Life

In Russia, Jewish children had for the most part gone only to Jewish schools. Schools of the Russian government were antisemitic and part of their program was to convert the Jews.

But the immigrants had no fear of the public school in America. They were filled with joy that their children could attend the public schools. In the old country there had been nothing like it. Few Jews were permitted to go to government schools in Eastern Europe, since there was a quota (a limit) on the number of Jews allowed to enter. Here in America, the schools were free and everybody had to attend. Most Jews were only too happy to go to school.

The mother of Jacob and Sarah dressed them as well as she could and sent them off proudly to school.

"Listen to the teacher. Have respect for the teacher." These words were repeated by father and mother. The children were excited by school and learned English quickly: After school hours, the children of immigrants would flock to the public libraries, another great wonder of America, to get books to read.

An immigrant family working at home, making artificial flowers. In poor families, all members, including children, helped to support the home. Very low wages were paid for such piecework.

In immigrant days school was compulsory* only to age fourteen, and some friends of Jacob and Sarah had to leave school early to go to work. Sometimes the wages of the oldest child would support

In a public school like this, immigrant children from many lands learned to speak and read English. For most, it was their introduction to America.

the family so that the younger children could go on to high school and even college.

Yankel and Sarah and their parents felt that they were lucky to live in New York. There were excellent high schools and there also were colleges that were free. At no cost, bright students could go to City College or Hunter College. From these schools came teachers, accountants, doctors, dentists, pharmacists, and lawyers.

Parents, after long hours of work, would go to school too. In evening classes they learned English and civics and American history, so that they could pass the tests to become citizens, after they had lived five years in America. But it

was not only at schools that the older people learned. They went to lectures and study groups of every kind, to meetings and discussions at settlement houses and YMHAs. There was a wide choice for the eager immigrants, for religious, socialist and Zionist groups held meetings for all ages.

In the settlement houses, immigrants learned the ways of America. But they still loved the culture and tradition of the old country. All the immigrants, both Jews and non-Jews, brought with them to America their language and customs, and their memories of home. They were often homesick, and liked to be with others who had come from the same place, to

Boys being weighed upon arrival at the Emma Farm Camp near Pittsburgh, one of the many institutions which tried to give summer recreation and healthful activity to children of poor immigrants.

talk the familiar language, sing the songs and even eat the foods of the old country.

The Jewish Love of Yiddish

There were foreign language newspapers for every nationality in America, German, Polish, Hungarian, Greek, and scores of others, many of them published in New York. The Jews of America, although smaller in total population, had an even greater number of newspapers and magazines than the others, published in Hebrew, Yiddish, or English. There was a weekly Yiddish newspaper in the United States as early as 1874. When many more Yiddish-speaking immigrants began to arrive in the 1880s, a number of daily newspapers began coming out. There were the *Tageblatt*, *The Daily Forward*, *The Day*, the *Morning Journal*, and many others.

The Yiddish papers offered not only news. There were columns about Jewish problems and ideals. There was information about American life, and articles to help the new citizen decide how to vote. There were even poems and novels in serial form. In 1916, half a million readers subscribed to Yiddish newspapers in the United States and Canada. No other foreign press was as large.

There were also Yiddish magazines of political or Zionist thought, or of prose and poetry, like *Die Zukunft*. Yiddish poets wrote about the life of the immigrant, memories of the past and hope for the future. There were novelists, storywriters and critics who wrote in Yiddish. Some, like I.J. Singer, Sholem Asch, and Sholem Aleichem, became known to readers of English as well, when their great works were translated.

Even more than the printed word, the spoken word of the Yiddish theater was dear to the Jewish immigrant's heart. Although there were millions of people in America who spoke foreign tongues, they did not develop a foreign-language theater in America that could compare in size or importance with the Yiddish stage

Mastheads of some of the Jewish Press in America, 1917–1918.

Sholem Aleichem (1859-1916), whose real name was Sholom Rabinowitz, most beloved of writers in Yiddish. He created many well-known characters, including Tevya the Dairyman. He wrote with humor and love of simple Jews in Europe and America.

of Second Avenue, on the Lower East Side of New York. The Yiddish plays and operettas that started in New York often went on tour to other cities of the United States, Canada, and South America.

Two plays which became classics in Yiddish and which were also popular in their English translations were Leivick's *Golem,* about the man-made monster who was supposed to help the Jews of Prague against their enemies in the Middle Ages; and Ansky's *The Dybbuk,* about a dead soul that returned to inhabit a living body. Some actors who got their start on the Yiddish stage went on to the English stage, and became famous on Broadway or in the movies.

Many Jewish Authors Wrote in English and Hebrew

There was, of course, much writing in English as well, on subjects of interest to Jewish readers. There was *The Menorah Journal* and other fine magazines. Most Jewish homes took at least one periodical that gave them news of fellow-Jews and writings by Jewish authors.

In 1888, a group of rabbis and scholars founded the Jewish Publication Society, which has published hundreds of books of Jewish interest. A great *Jewish Encycolopedia* was put out in 1906 and forty years later another, called *Universal Jewish Encyclopedia,* was published.

There are also Hebrew books and magazines in America. A famous magazine is *Hadoar,* a Hebrew weekly. There have been Hebrew poets and scholars who were also great teachers in schools of higher Jewish learning.

Jews are known in America as lovers of

Albert Einstein (1879–1955) the geat Jewish physicist who developed the "theory of relativity", for which he was awarded the Nobel Prize in 1921. A refugee from Nazi Germany, he settled in the United States and was active on behalf of many Jewish causes.

learning. Education, both religious and general, has been a top concern of Jewish parents. Love of learning was an old tradition that Jewish immigrants brought with them. America permitted this tradition to flower.

Many American Jews have become great scholars. Some have won Nobel prizes in science. Others have become leading doctors, writers, musicians and artists, lawyers and judges. Jews are also among the leading supporters of art and music and other cultural activities in their communities.

Felix Warburg (1871–1937) Jewish banker and philanthropist. He was chairman of the American Joint Distribution Committee from 1914–1932. He was active on behalf of the Jewish Theological Seminary of America, the Hebrew Union College and Zionist causes.

Adolph Ochs (1858–1935) developed the *New York Times* into one of the world's most influential newspapers.

David Sarnoff (1891–1971) who began as a messenger boy and wireless operator. He rose to become head of the Radio Corporation of America. He was active on behalf of Jewish causes.

CHAPTER XIV

Caring For Their Brothers

In the Book of Esther which we read on Purim, Mordecai asks Queen Esther to go to the king and save her people. "Who can say?" he urges her. "Maybe you were raised to the king's court just so that you could help your people."

Jews who have been in a position to help have often tried to give aid to their people. In free America, Jews have been able as never before to speak out and ask justice for fellow Jews suffering persecution. They have also befriended their less fortunate brethren all over the world.

New York, May 8th, 1903.

Dear Sir :—

Great distress prevails at Kischineff, Russia, by reason of the Anti-Semitic riots last week, wherein we are informed that more than one hundred persons of the Jewish faith were killed, from five to six hundred were injured, and many others were made homeless and suffered the destruction of their property. The *Alliance Israélite Universelle* has cabled requesting our co-operation in securing financial relief, stating that several million francs are needed for this purpose. After a discussion of the situation, we believe that this community should co-operate liberally with the *Alliance Israélite* in providing relief; and your subscription is therefore solicited. In view of the necessities of the case, you are urged to send promptly whatever contribution you may desire to make, to MR. DANIEL GUGGENHEIM, Treasurer of the Relief Fund, 71 Broadway, New York City.

Yours truly,

EMANUEL LEHMAN, Chairman,　　LOUIS MARSHALL,
NATHAN BIJUR,　　　　　　　　HENRY RICE,
JOSEPH B. BLOOMINGDALE,　　JACOB H. SCHIFF,
SIMON BORG,　　　　　　　　　ISAAC N. SELIGMAN,
DANIEL GUGGENHEIM,　　　　　LOUIS STERN,
CHARLES L. HALLGARTEN,　　ISIDOR STRAUS,
MYER S. ISAACS,　　　　　　　CYRUS L. SULZBERGER,
MORRIS LOEB,　　　　　　　　ISAAC WALLACH.

A plea for funds on behalf of the victims of the Kishinev pogrom.

Benjamin Franklin Peixotto (1834-1890) leading Jewish citizen who was president of B'nai B'rith, consul to Bucharest, Rumania, and consul also in France. In Rumania he tried to help persecuted Jews.

Though there has always been some antisemitism in America, presidents and Congress have most often acted favorably towards Jewish causes. An example was President Grant's appointing Benjamin Peixotto, a Jew, as Ambassador to Rumania, at a time when there was much antisemitism in that country.

Non-Jewish citizens have frequently joined with Jews in protesting incidents of anti-Jewish violence abroad. Christians joined with Jews in 1903, for instance, to denounce a pogrom at Kishinev, a city in Eastern Europe. In that year, on the day after Easter, forty-seven Jews were killed and hundreds injured. President Theodore Roosevelt agreed to send a protest to the czar.

There were more pogroms after the Revolution of 1905 failed in Russia. Our Congress unanimously adopted a resolution condemning the slaughter. Leading Jewish philanthropists, Oscar Straus and Jacob Schiff, headed a committee that raised over a million dollars for Jewish relief.

A few years later, the civilized world, including many American churchmen, was shocked at the reviving of the blood libel by Russian prosecutors in the Mendel Beilis case in Kiev, Russia, in 1911. Mr. Beilis, a poor Russian worker, was accused of having killed a Christian to use his blood. Christians and Jews the world over protested and Beilis was eventually set free.

Am I My Brother's Keeper?

Jews have everywhere set an example in caring for the needy and helpless among them. In many cities of the United

A reporter's drawing of Mendel Beilis on trial in Russia on the trumped-up charge of ritual slaughter. People all over the world protested this antisemitic scandal.

States and Canada, Jewish hospitals, orphan homes, old people's homes, and charitable and loan societies have been set up as soon as enough Jews came together in a town or city.

Jews willingly supported these and other institutions. In Philadelphia, soon after the Civil War, the United Hebrew Charities was formed. This brought together many of the city's Jewish charity organizations, so they would make only one fund drive in the city. Then all the agencies would share what the people contributed. In the Jewish community such a united appeal may be called Federation or Welfare Fund. The system is used now also in the general community, under the name Community Chest or United Fund.

Jewish organizations dedicated to philanthropy and other good causes were also social groups. Here is a Purim Ball at the Academy of Music in New York in 1865.

Many wealthy Jews became famous for their philanthropy. Nathan Straus, who gave much money for Jewish causes in America, Russia and Palestine, was also noted for his work in getting a law for pasteurizing milk passed. This saved many lives. Julius Rosenwald also gave to Jewish causes and, in addition, gave a great deal of money to establish and help

Jacob H. Schiff (1847-1920), outstanding Jewish philanthropist. He gave support to universities, hospitals, and cultural activities both Jewish and general, helping religious institutions of all groups. His firm would not lend money to Czarist Russia because of its persecution of the Jews.

Negro schools and colleges. Another great philanthropist was Jacob Schiff, who helped support a variety of Jewish institutions, as well as many of the country's universities. Felix Warburg, his son-in-law, followed his example, making contributions also for general cultural activities.

Such men were among the leaders who founded the American Jewish Committee in 1906 and the Anti-Defamation League of B'nai B'rith in 1913, to work for the civil and religious rights of Jews in any part of the world, and to help Jewish victims of persecutions.

When World War I broke out in 1914, millions of European Jews, especially Russian Jews, suffered because they lived in the path of battle. American Jews set up a relief committee, with Louis Marshall, a leading lawyer, as chairman. This soon expanded and became the now famous American Jewish Joint Distribution Committee. This agency was called either the "Joint" or JDC. It became a great network for lifesaving activities all over the world. During and after the war, its workers helped refugees,* provided medical aid when there were epidemics, rebuilt schools, and rehabilitated* lives. Its work continues to this day in Europe, North

Africa, and wherever Jews are in need.

To make possible the magnificent work of the JDC, the Jews of America gave $6,000,000 in 1916, $10,000,000 in 1917, and more in years thereafter. Money given for the United Jewish Appeal today goes in part to this cause.

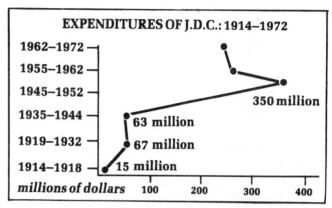

The Joint Distribution Committee has been the most remarkable and far-reaching of all private philanthropies, feeding, rescuing, training, and re-settling persecuted Jews all over the world. The amount given by Jews of the democratic countries for JDC activities has increased as the need has grown greater.

A Time of Trouble for Jews

The American Jewish community sent delegates to the Peace Conference held by France, England, and the United States after the First World War. They asked for minority* rights and guaranteed freedoms for Jews in every country of Europe. This was promised in the Versailles Treaty that ended the war. A League of Nations was formed after the war, which was supposed to safeguard these minority rights, for Jews as well as non-Jews.

The Jewish delegations of the United States and of European countries also asked for a guarantee that the Balfour Declaration of 1917, which promised a home for the Jewish people in Palestine, would be carried out. This matter was put in the hands of the League, and England was given the mandate* over Palestine to see that the promise was fulfilled.

129

The Balfour Declaration, declaring that the British government viewed with favor the establishment of a national home for the Jewish people in Palestine, issued in 1917.

Many problems for the Jews lay ahead, however. In Poland, which took over the rule of a province where two million Jews lived, antisemitism grew rapidly. The rights of Jews that had been guaranteed by the Versailles Treaty were simply disregarded in that country, and also in Rumania and elsewhere. Antisemitism spread like a cancer in many parts of Europe in the years after the war.

A cartoon showing the relationship of the Czarist Russian government to the Jews.

The situation of the Jews in Russia was uncertain for a time. Things looked good following the Communist Revolution of 1917, for the new government promised equality to all national groups, and tolerance for all. Many Jews were hopeful of a better day, since they were accepted as a national minority. However, the history of pogroms and persecutions in Russia, and the fact that the new regime attacked all religions, made people unsure as to whether Jews would be really free under Russian Communism.

Troubled and fearful for the future, many Jews of Russia and Poland wanted to come to America, but it was no longer as easy as it had been in the previous fifty years. The United States had needed and welcomed immigrants then, but feeling grew in the 1920s against further large-scale immigration to the United States.

Members of the Committee on Immigration of the House of Representatives received by members of the board of directors of The Hebrew Sheltering and Immigrant Aid Society of America, at 229 E. Broadway, New York City, on November 25, 1919.

Many of the people who were against immigration were bigots who hated foreigners, but there were also workers and labor leaders who wanted fewer immigrants. Business and trade was bad after the war, and there was fear that immigrants would work for low wages. Employers would take advantage of this to hire the newcomers and fire the older workers. The so-called "native" workers therefore joined in the anti-immigration movement that swept the country in those years. Many also worried that foreigners from Europe, especially those from Eastern Europe and the poorer countries, would bring communist ideas into the country with them.

A strong anti-immigration law was passed in 1924. This greatly reduced the number who could enter the United States from countries of eastern and southern Europe. The law discriminated against Greeks, Italians, Poles, Hungarians, Russians, and Jews, but favored people who came from northern Europe, the so-called "Nordics*" from England, Germany and Scandinavia.

The Immigration Act of 1924 turned out to be a very unfortunate law for the Jews. Before it was passed, 140,000 Jews had come in one year After the law only about 10,000 a year were permitted into the United States. Many, many more thousands of Jews from eastern and southern Europe would have come, for conditions had become unsafe for them. But the American escape route was closed. Hundreds of thousands of Jews

This photograph shows some of the results of the work of resettlement done by the United Jewish Appeal. Old and young newcomers are being helped off the gangplank of a ship that has come from Europe to Haifa, Israel.

might have been able to flee from Hitler's clutches, when the Nazis came to power a short decade later, and the pitiless slaughter of Europe's Jews began.

American Jews did what they could to help, but they could not rescue all their people in Europe.

Armed Ku Klux Klansmen dressed in hooded robes were an "invisible empire" in the South. At its peak the Klan had about four million members. Klan meetings were always opened by the burning of a huge cross. Many murders, whippings and tarrings were committed by the Klan. Membership was limited to "native white Protestants".

Anti-immigrant and anti-foreigner feeling grew strong in America in the twentieth century. The Ku Klux Klan, which was primarily anti-Negro, but hated Jews, Catholics and foreigners as well, gained power in the South and other parts of the country. In 1920, Henry Ford aided the antisemitic cause by reprinting in his newspaper a forgery called *The Protocols of the Elders of Zion*, a made-up story accusing the Jews of secretly planning to rule the world.

CHAPTER XV

Looking Towards Zion

America is made up of people from many lands. There are Italo-Americans, Polish-Americans, German-Americans, Irish-Americans, Afro-Americans—each of these can be said to make up an ethnic group. Usually the people of such a group feel a special interest in the culture, the language, the songs and folk tales and customs, the past glories of their people or their country of origin.

American citizens can also be grouped according to their religon. There are Catholics, a great many Protestant sects, Jews, Moslems, Buddhists, and others. The Jews are in an unusual situation, however. They are both a religious and an ethnic or cultural group.

Besides their religious laws and beliefs and prayers, Jews also share a common history. Catholics or Protestants may share a common religion, but if they come from England, France or Germany, they do not share a common history. The Jews of England, France and Germany, however, do have a common background. Jews have a common place of origin, they have their original language, Hebrew, that they

brought from ancient Palestine, and they have the tongue they developed in Europe, Yiddish. They share the Bible, and the memory of the Exodus and the Babylonian Exile and a great many events of history, as well as a considerable literature in both languages. Wherever they lived they developed a special kind of community life, one that combined customs, religious holidays and practices, and traditions based on the teachings of the rabbis.

Jews Have a Special Interest in Israel

Like Irish-Americans who are interested in the problems of Ireland, or Italo-Americans who collect money to help flood victims in Italy, Jews in America feel a special closeness to other Jews all over the world. As American citizens they are concerned with all the problems America faces, but they also have a deep interest in the well-being of the Jewish homeland of Israel, and in the problems of Jews in other lands.

Americans, Gentiles as well as Jews,

have always shown interest in the "Promised Land." Warder Cresson, a wealthy Philadelphian, converted to Judaism and settled in Jerusalem in 1848. He tried to introduce new methods of farming to help restore the land. Clorinda Minor established a Christian farm colony near where Tel Aviv stands today, called Mount Hope. A minister, William Blackstone, asked President Harrison in 1891 "to consider the condition of the Israelites and their claims to Palestine as their ancient home."

American Jews of traditional faith, like all Jews before them, said prayers in their daily worship for the rebuilding of Zion, and at the end of each Passover *seder** expressed the wish, "Next year in Jerusalem." This thought had helped the persecuted Jews of all lands to look to the future with hope through the ages.

Many Jews who prospered in America tried to do something to make the wish come true. Mordecai Manuel Noah planned his City of Refuge as a stopping place on the way to Palestine. Judah Touro left his largest bequest to be used by Moses Montefiore for the Jews in Jerusalem.

The idea that Jews might settle and build up the land by themselves, rather than wait for the help of the Messiah, grew strong in the last century. Most of the immigrant Jews had great interest and sympathy with the idea of "the Return."

In 1897, when Theodor Herzl called the first Zionist Congress in Basel, Switzerland, there were no official delegates from America. There did exist, however, some Zionist feeling in the country. There was, for instance, a group called the Knights of Zion. It is interesting that one of its founders was Bernhard Felsenthal, a Reform rabbi, for the Reform movement

Zionist leaders: Dr. Max Bodenheimer, Theodor Herzl, Dr. Max Nordau, and David Wolfssohn.

as a whole was at that time not in sympathy with the Zionist belief in the Jews as a nation whose rightful home was in Palestine. By and large, "old-line" Reform Jews believed that the Jews were scattered in different countries of the world because they had a "mission" to spread the knowledge of one God. They could make their homeland wherever they were permitted to live freely and openly as Jews.

There were many Jews, in America and elsewhere, who were not in favor of Zionism. Many wealthy Jews were uncomfortable about the teachings of political Zionism. They were at ease in America, and did not want to be accused of loyalty to some other state.

There was opposition, also, from poorer people, and from leftist* and radical* Jews who hoped to change society so *all* people could have a better life. Such Jews generally wanted men and women to think of themselves as workers and human beings, not as Jews or Catholics or Protestants—or for that matter as Americans, Germans, French, or of any particular nation. Even though they were themselves Jews, they did not want to concern themselves with the special problems of Jews. They believed that all problems would be solved after "the Revolution."

There were Jews who had the socialist ideals of the "leftists" but who nevertheless believed in working for a Jewish state. Nahman Syrkin was one of them. The leader of the *Poale Zion* (Workers of Zion) group which began in New York in 1903, he dreamed of establishing the ideal society within the Jewish state.

Most Jews who had come to America after 1881 wished to see a Jewish homeland rebuilt. Many of them, however, would not support the Zionist movement, for most Zionist leaders were not religious. Some pious folk believed it was not right to try to regain the land of Israel through human effort. It was necessary to wait for the Messiah.

Among Orthodox Jews, however, there were many who wished to work for the Jewish state. They formed the *Mizrachi* party in 1902. In America, Meyer Berlin was the leader. He felt that observant Jews could work for a Jewish state that would be true to Jewish tradition. The name of the group can mean "Of the East," but is formed from an abbreviation of Hebrew words meaning "spiritual center."

There was considerable Zionist feeling in America, for in 1898, soon afer the first Zionist congress, nearly 100 groups set up a Federation of American Zionists in New York. Other groups joined it later. The Federation held conventions and tried to educate Jews and other Americans to the Zionist point of view.

Stephen S. Wise, a young Reform rabbi who later became known as the most brilliant of all American Jewish orators, was first secretary of the Federation. He had refused to become rabbi of the largest Reform temple in the country, Emanu-El of New York, because he knew they would not let him preach his Zionist ideas.

Another leader of the Federation was Louis Lipsky of Rochester. A writer, debater and organizer, he edited the monthly Zionist magazine, *The Maccabean*, for many years, and chaired the annual conventions for many years. The Federation later became the Zionist Organization of America.

Leaders in the American Zionist Movement

The religious group that gave most support for Zionism was the Conservative movement. From the beginning, this group spoke of the fact that the Jews were a people with common hopes and a

Rabbi Stephen S. Wise, Rabbi Israel Goldstein and Louis Lipsky.

Hadassah Hospital in Jerusalem.

founded by Henrietta Szold, a scholar and editor. After a trip to Palestine in 1909, when she was fifty years old, Miss Szold decided that what the Jews there needed most were health care and education. She persuaded Nathan Straus to give enough money for a medical unit to be sent to Palestine in 1913.

After the War, Hadassah women supplied health and medical care and relief to the people of the Yishuv. Tremendous sums were raised by Jewish women in America, and Arabs as well as Jews were helped by Hadassah in Palestine. Aided by these sums, doctors were able to put an end to trachoma, the age-old eye disease of the Middle East, and malaria. In time the organization built the Hadassah Hospital in Jerusalem, which was made part of the Hebrew University.

Miss Szold went to Palestine to help set

culture that united them. Rabbi Solomon Schechter, who had been called from Cambridge University in England in 1902 to head the Jewish Theological Seminary, founded the United Synagogue of America, which supported the Zionist cause.

"Young Judea," one of the groups that made up the General Zionists, was an organization for boys and girls. Young Judeans learned Hebrew songs, danced horas, and studied the history of the *Yishuv,** the Jewish community that was growing up in Palestine. First president of the General Zionists was the teacher Israel Friedlaender, who was killed by bandits in 1920 while he was bringing relief to Jews in the Ukraine after the Russian Revolution.

An American group which did more practical work than any other in the land of Palestine is Hadassah, the Women's Zionist Organization of America. It was

Solomon Schechter (1860-1915), scholar of Eastern Europe, Germany, and England, called from Cambridge University to head the Jewish Theological Seminary of America in 1902. He gathered the great faculty and library of the Seminary, and gave form to the Conservative movement.

135

up clinics and administer the activities of Hadassah. Her last job was to head "Youth *Aliyah,*"" the rescue campaign that specialized in saving children from Hitler's Europe.

Hadassah has continued as the largest organization of Jewish women and the most successful of all Zionist groups.

When World War I began, a new leader came to American Zionism, Louis D. Brandeis. He became chairman of a committee for the Jews of Palestine. His committee sent millions of dollars of relief funds to Palestine, and also to suffering Jews in Russia and Rumania.

Brandeis, born in Louisville, Kentucky, had been influenced by his uncle, Lewis Dembitz, a religious Jew and Zionist, and by Theodor Herzl's friend, Jacob de Haas. He felt that Zionism was the greatest cause for which an America Jew could work.

Louis Dembitz Brandeis (1856-1941), Justice of the Supreme Court and Zionist leader. A champion of liberal causes, he became interested in Judaism and Zionism when he met Jewish garment workers during settlement of a strike in 1910. He said that following Jewish ideals made one a better American.

The 39th (British) Battalion, in which Jews fought for liberation of Palestine during World War I, camped outside Jerusalem.

136

Jewish citizens who did not favor Zionism were amazed when Brandeis said, "To be good Americans we must be better Jews, and to be better Jews we must become Zionists." He said that "American ideals have been Jewish ideals for twenty centuries." For him there was no such thing as conflict between his Americanism and Zionism.

In 1916, President Wilson appointed Brandeis a justice of the Supreme Court, the highest government position to which any Jew thus far has been able to rise in the United States. It is a curious thing that there were Jews, among others, who fought against his appointment. Some Jewish businessmen thought he was too liberal, while other Jews worried that if he did something unpopular, all Jews would be blamed. Brandeis was a distinguished justice of the Supreme Court for over twenty years, but he kept up his work for Jewish rights in America, and helped make it possible for the Yishuv in Palestine to grow in industry and income.

American Jews did their share in working for the rebuilding of the homeland. Many became part of a Jewish legion of volunteers who joined England during World War I, before the United States entered the war, to fight the Turks who ruled Palestine. Zionists all over the world rejoiced when Palestine became a mandated* territory under British administration after the First World War. They felt that England would do a good job in seeing that the Jewish state would soon become a reality. But there were many problems ahead, as we shall see.

CHAPTER XVI

Their Place In America

A family sat one evening in the living room of their comfortable apartment on the Grand Concourse in the Bronx. The grandfather and grandmother were visiting, but no one seemed happy.

The daughter of the family was speaking.

"Tomorrow I'll go looking again," she said. "So far I've had no luck."

"It's the Depression," said the father. "There are so many people out of work. No wonder you can't get a job." This was in the 1930s.

"I know," said the daughter. "But it's also very obvious that the personnel manager at the store decided he didn't want me when he saw that I had put down my religion as Jewish on the application blank. And at the telephone company, my friend was told that Jews were not hired as operators because they wouldn't get along well with the other girls."

"Someday they won't ask your religion," said the mother. "It doesn't seem to be a democratic thing to do."

"If only they wouldn't ask for religion on the medical school applications," said the son. "I'm second in my college class. Some of the men who were much lower have already heard that they've been accepted by good schools like Harvard and Johns Hopkins. I haven't heard yet."

"But you must go to medical school," said his sister. "You would be a wonderful doctor."

The brother smiled sadly. "Maybe I'll go to the University of Glasgow Medical School. My friend Sam was able to go there when none of the American schools accepted him."

The grandfather spoke. "I always wished that my children and grandchildren would do better than I . Some of my dreams have come true. Your father owns a business instead of working as a pants presser the way I did. And you children have gotten a good education."

"Yes," said the grandmother, "and you live now in such a nice apartment, not like the place where we lived on Hester Street."

"Of course things are better, if you compare it with what you had to put up with," said the father. "But my children and I are Americans. This is the land of equality. There shouldn't be the kind of antisemitism my children are finding."

"The colleges call it 'quotas,'" said the grandson. "They say they only want to

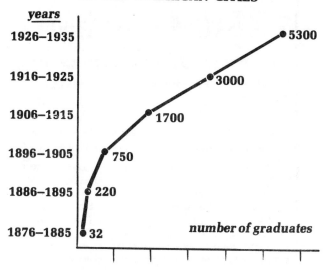

JEWISH GRADUATES OF MEDICAL SCHOOLS IN TEN AMERICAN CITIES

years

1926–1935	● 5300
1916–1925	● 3000
1906–1915	● 1700
1896–1905	● 750
1886–1895	● 220
1876–1885	● 32

number of graduates

Jewish graduates of medical schools in ten American cities. It was well known that for many years medical schools discriminated against admission of Jews, allowing only a certain percentage, or quota, of Jewish students in each class.

keep a proper balance. What they really want is a big majority of white Anglo-Saxon Protestants. That's their idea of what America is. Jews, Italians, Negroes, people with foreign-sounding names—people like us don't count. They have only a limited number of places for us."

"But don't forget, son, we're not sitting by idly," said the father. "We are fighting against this. We have an Anti-Defamation League, the American Jewish Congress, the American Jewish Committee—a number of organizations are working against it. They are taking cases to court and getting congressmen to vote for bills against this kind of discrimination.*"

"When laws are passed against discrimination, not only the Jews will be helped," said the mother. "Everyone will be, and America as a whole will be stronger, because there will be doctors and people in every field who are there because they deserve it, not because their religion or skin is the correct one."

"Till that time, though," said the son, "America may miss out on some pretty good doctors."

"I wish I had gone into teaching," said the daughter. "But even there some of my friends were told they couldn't be accepted because they had 'foreign accents.' But at least in jobs that are given by the government, like teaching and Civil Service, there is less discrimination."

"When I hear from the last medical school," said the son, "I may take the exam for post office clerk. There, at least, if you pass an exam, you get a job."

Antisemitism Never Really Dies

In the 1930s and 1940s, American Jews were no longer poor immigrants trying to find their place in a strange land. Most had been raised in this country and felt at home in America. All they wanted was the right to work in their chosen field. Many did manage to become successful, but practically every Jew living in America in the thirties knew of antisemitism at home as well as abroad.

Sometimes the discrimination was not too harmful. There were clubs, restaurants and hotels that did not admit Jews. There were many places where people

The center-spread of *Life* (May 12, 1910) carried the antisemitic cartoon entitled "The Surrender of New York." It pictures the people of New York surrendering their city to Jewish merchants.

lived that were called "restricted." This meant that it was a waste of time for Jews, or Negroes, or sometimes even Catholics, to try to buy a house or rent an apartment in those areas. Some excuse would be found not to rent or sell homes to such people. And before laws were finally passed to stop the practice, newspapers printed advertisements for jobs which said plainly that Jews or Negroes, or whatever group the employer didn't like, need not apply.

Sometimes there was violent antisemitism as well. Some groups like the "Christian Mobilizers" made speeches on street corners against Jews and sold antisemitic papers on the street. Often fights were started and some Jews were beaten up. Things began to get worse in the Thirties when Nazism rose to power in Germany. Hate groups in this country then became more active.

Advertisement of one of the many vicious antisemitic fringe groups that have grown up in this country.

The fact that Seligman was an outstanding citizen and friend of President Grant made his being turned away at a hotel more newsworthy than the common run of antisemitic incidents.

Nevertheless, Jews Made Progress in America

Most Americans understood that bigotry was not the American way. The founders of the country and all its presidents had believed in the equality of all men. The elected officials of the government were friendly toward the Jews, as was shown when Congress unanimously passed a resolution favoring the establishment of a homeland in Palestine for the Jewish people.

In America, in spite of antisemitism, Jews in large numbers were able to get good educations, and through hard work, to succeed in their jobs. Many Jewish families, like the one on the Grand Concourse in the Bronx, had at first been supported in this country by a father who was a garment worker or a peddler who raised himself up to storekeeper. From such humble beginnings came some leaders in business and professions. There were Jewish poor and Jews in the middle class, but also some who rose to great wealth in industry, like the Guggenheims, Littauers and Lewisohns.

There were advances for Jews in other fields as well. Medicine and healing had always been interests of the Jew. It is impossible to list all the Jewish physi-

cians who became important in America, but those who were outstanding in research include Dr. Joseph Goldberger, who discovered the cause and cure of pellagra; Dr. Casimir Funk, who discovered vitamins; Dr. Bela Schick, who developed the test for diphtheria; Dr. Selman Waksman who received the Nobel Prize for his work in antibiotics; Drs. Jonas Salk and Albert Sabin, who developed vaccines against polio.

Joseph Pulitzer (1847–1911), leading newspaper publisher, who endowed the Columbia School of Journalism and left money for the giving of the annual Pulitzer prizes for outstanding journalists, writers, and composers.

Jews are numbered among America's great scientists. The Nobel Prize in Chemistry was won by Harold Urey, and Nobel Prizes in Physics were won by Albert Michelson, Isidor Rabi, and the greatest of scientists, Albert Einstein, who became an American citizen when he had to flee Nazi Germany.

Thousands of Jews have contributed much in art, music and the theater. There have been sculptors and artists, composers and song-writers, singers, instrumentalists and conductors. A high percentage of the great pianists and violinists are Jews.

In the theater, there are Jews among playwrights, actors, producers and crit-

Albert Sabin, research scientist who developed the oral polio vaccine, and president of the Weizmann Institute of Science at Rehovot, Israel.

Arthur J. Goldberg, chief of the United States delegation to the United Nations, Secretary of Labor, 1961–1962, Associate Justice of the United States Supreme Court, 1962–1965.

Jews have not been alone in the struggle against antisemitism. Most Americans were shocked by the terrible results of antisemitism in Nazi Europe. During World War II there were laws passed to end discrimination in jobs. Colleges and universities began to discard their quota systems. Housing became much more open, although not so open for blacks. Many clubs that excluded Jews and other minorities had to give up the practice. Jews have been able to become engineers and college professors in large numbers, and to find work in other fields where they used to meet discrimination.

In a more open* society, Jews are more than ever able to follow wherever their talents and interests lead them.

ics. Many Jews have become famous as comedians. Jews were particularly important in the development of the movies, an entertainment field that they helped start in the 1920s. In those days this industry required originality and daring but not much money. There have been outstanding Jewish athletes in boxing, baseball, basketball and football. Listing the names of all Jews who have made worthy contributions would take many pages.

Benjamin Cardozo and Felix Frankfurter followed Brandeis in being appointed to the Supreme Court. There are Jewish judges on every level throughout the country. There have been many congressmen and senators, including Simon Guggenheim, Benjamin Jonas, Herbert Lehman and Jacob Javits, and governors of many states. Jews have been advisers to presidents, cabinet members and ambassadors.

Benjamin Cardozo (1870–1938) was a Justice of the Supreme Court of the United States, where he served with distinction. He was noted for a humane approach to the law.

CHAPTER XVII

With Heart And Hand

Jews of America answered "Yes" to the question "Am I my brother's keeper?" With their limited power, they tried to warn America about the dangers of Nazism to all the free world, and to help their brethren escape from Germany and the other countries of Europe that came under Nazi rule.

As early as 1933, when Hitler came to power in Germany, the American Jewish Congress called for demonstrations against Nazism. Madison Square Garden in New York was the scene of the largest rally, and there were three thousand other meetings throughout the land.

Christians as well as Jews joined in the Nonsectarian Anti-Nazi League to Champion Human Rights. Many began to boycott German goods. In Germany, Jews were deprived of rights, books by Jewish authors were burned, and synagogues were destroyed.

The Struggle to Save Jewish Lives

At the beginning of Nazi persecution, Jews were still able to leave Germany. However, immigration to the United States was limited by the immigration laws, and the number that could enter Palestine was also limited. Jews in the United States worked hard to persuade the two governments to admit more refugees, but only a small number were helped.

The Joint Distribution Committee continued its work of helping Jews in Europe

A call to a demonstration against antisemitic terror in Poland in 1932. American students and others protested persecution of fellow-Jews in countries of Europe. The next year, Hitler came to power in Germany. Mass meetings were attended by hundreds of thousands of American Jews.

This famous photograph, taken from German archives, shows Nazi soldiers rounding up "the enemy" in the Warsaw ghetto. The last survivors, almost unarmed, held off an armored Nazi division for many days in the heroic Battle of the Warsaw ghetto.

as long as it could, but by 1938 the Nazi influence had spread to most of the continent. It was almost impossible for Jews to help their brethren any longer. The Jews of Europe were trapped, but most of the world did not protest or try to stop the Nazis in any way. In 1939 Germany invaded Poland. World War II had begun.

Helpless to send any aid into the war-torn continent, Jews of America could not even get information as to what was going on. The bits of news that were smuggled out of the areas occupied by the Nazis indicated that the local populations of each country the Germans conquered joined with the Nazis to oppress and kill Jews. Many people could not believe that Germany, a civilized and Christian country, could do such things. But after the war ended in 1945 the appalling truth came out that fully six million Jews had

been done to death in the concentration camps of Hitler's Europe.

Many of the camps were liberated by American troops. There were some survivors, who came to be called Displaced Persons (or D.P.s). They were cared for mainly by American soldiers. Jewish chaplains helped, and Jewish relief agencies sent in food. The desire of most

The Warsaw Ghetto aflame. Thousands of Jews burned to death rather than surrender to the Nazis.

The Exodus, ship of the Haganah, which carried 4500 Jewish refugees to Palestine from the Displaced Persons camps of Europe following World War II. The British, still holding the Mandate over Palestine, refused to allow the ship to dock, and returned it to Hamburg. This helped swing world opinion towards the creation of a Jewish State.

then limiting Jewish immigration to Palestine. The British government had declared in 1939, when there was a last chance for the escape of a substantial number of Jews of Europe, that immigration of Jews to Palestine must stop entirely, so that Jews would not outnumber Arabs.

Jews in America and England made strong protests. Many of them, aroused by the terrible fate of so many of their people, joined the Zionist movement and organized many demonstrations. England finally, after the war against Germany ended, said that the problem of the Jewish state should be given to the United Nations for a vote.

The Birth of Israel

Debates went on in the United Nations. Besides representatives of the Yishuv itself, the chief spokesman for the Jewish cause in America was Abba Hillel Silver, a Reform rabbi who headed the American

survivors was to go to the only land where they would feel safe and the people would welcome them, Palestine.

The Yishuv there had been growing between the two wars, from 53,000 to about half a million. But England was

THE PALESTINE POST

JERUSALEM
SUNDAY, MAY 16, 1948

PRICE: 25 MILS
VOL. XXIII. No. 6714

STATE OF ISRAEL IS BORN

The first independent Jewish State in 19 centuries was born in Tel Aviv as the British Mandate over Palestine came to an end at midnight on Friday, and it was immediately subjected to the test of fire. As "Medinat Yisrael" (State of Israel) was proclaimed, the battle for Jerusalem raged, with most of the city falling to the Jews. At the same time, President Truman announced that the United States would accord recognition to the new State. A few hours later, Palestine was invaded by Moslem armies from the south, east and north, and Tel Aviv was raided from the air. On Friday the United Nations Special Assembly adjourned after adopting a resolution to appoint a mediator but without taking any action on the Partition Resolution of November 29.

Yesterday the battle for the Jerusalem-Tel Aviv road was still under way, and two Arab villages were taken. In the north, Acre town was captured, and the Jewish Army consolidated its positions in Western Galilee.

Most Crowded Hours in Palestine's History

Between Thursday night and this morning Palestine went through what by all standards must be among the most crowded hours in its history.

For the Jewish population there was the anguish over the fate of the few hundred Haganah men and women in the Kfar Etzion bloc of settlements near Hebron. Their

JEWS TAKE OVER SECURITY ZONES

The Battle for Jerusalem, which began when the British forces withdrew on Friday morning, continued all day Friday and yesterday. The crackle of small-arms fire and explosions of mortar shells

Egyptian Air Force Spitfires Bomb Tel Aviv; One Shot Down

Kol Israel, the Tel Aviv broadcasting station, reported at 2 o'clock yesterday afternoon that Tel Aviv had been bombed three times in the previous evening and morning, and that one plane had been

A country-wide blackout was ordered by Air Raid Precaution Headquarters in Tel Aviv.

Mr. David Ben Gurion, the Prime Minister, broadcast from Tel Aviv to the people

U.S. RECOGNIZES JEWISH STATE

WASHINGTON, Saturday.
—Ten minutes after the termination of the British Mandate on Friday, the White House released a formal statement by President Truman that the U.S. Gov-

Proclamation by Head Of Government

The creation of "Medinat Yisrael", the State of Israel, was proclaimed at midnight on Friday by Mr. David Ben Gurion, until then Chairman of the Jewish Agency Executive and now head of the State's Provisional Council of Government.

The first act of the Council

The jubilant first page of the English-language newspaper of Israel (now called the *Jerusalem Post*), proclaiming the birth of the new state, which occurred May 14, 1948.

section of the Jewish Agency. The Arab leaders were against any Jewish state at all, and it was widely said that companies with oil interests in Arab lands were working behind the scenes to line up the American government on the side of the Arabs.

On November 29, 1947, Jews of America and all the world listened to their radios as the final vote in the United Nations was broadcast. One nation after another was called, and answered yes, no or abstain. The United States voted yes; the Soviet Union also said yes. At the end of the vote, the General Assembly stood 33 for, 13 against, and 10 abstained.

Jews everywhere rejoiced. There was finally to be a Jewish state once again! A Jewish state with its own government, one that would allow all Jews to enter who wished to become settlers.

The British left Palestine on the agreed date, on May 14, 1948. The State of Israel was proclaimed, but there was no peace. The Arab nations invaded the newly declared state immediately after the British left. The United States recognized the new nation immediately, but at the same time said that it would be neutral in the conflict. No arms would be sent from the U.S. to the Middle East. There were Jews who smuggled some arms to Palestine, and some went there to fight themselves. Fortunately, Czechoslovakia sold Israel arms and eventually the Jews of Israel were able to force the Arabs to accept a cease fire. This enabled Israel to begin to build up the country.

President Truman and the American people as a whole were sympathetic to the new state. But it was the Jews of America who cared most and who continued to accept the responsibility to help Israel grow strong. Besides giving to the UJA to help immigration and resettlement, they have lent the government money through buying Israel bonds. Donors from the United States and from other great Jewish communities of England, Canada, South Africa and Argentina, have helped build up universities, the Technion, the Weizmann Institute, and schools and institutions of every kind.

CHAPTER XVIII

Modern Times

About six million Jews now live in the United States. They still live in or near the larger cities. Many live in the suburbs that have grown up around the cities since World War II. Although in 1971 and '72 there were about a half million Jews in the poverty class, most Jews are considered as part of the middle class. They do every type of work, and there is very little discrimination against them. A high percentage of them are business executives, professional or skilled people.

There continue to be many Jews in music, art, theater and literature. Most striking has been the number of outstanding Jewish novelists in the 50s and 60s. Education and philanthropy, which can be called "Torah" and "good deeds," continue to be top interests of American Jews.

Jews Remain Devoted to Education

Elementary Hebrew schools have raised their standards and Hebrew high schools have increased, among Reform as well as Conservative and Orthodox congregations. Many children now go to Hebrew Day Schools. There are hundreds of such schools, teaching general as well as Jewish subjects, most organized by the Orthodox, but a growing number sponsored by Conservative groups and some by Reform Jews.

In higher education, Jews have also made strides. Yeshiva University has expanded, adding graduate schools, Stern College for Women and Einstein Medical College. Its rabbinical department, the Isaac Elchanan Theological Seminary, ordains Orthodox rabbis, as do some other yeshivot.

The Jewish Theological Seminary of

COLLEGE AND UNIVERSITY TEACHERS:

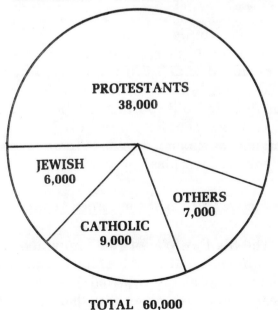

PROTESTANTS
38,000

JEWISH
6,000

OTHERS
7,000

CATHOLIC
9,000

TOTAL 60,000

Yeshiva University in New York, Orthodox institution which includes high schools, undergraduate colleges for men and women, graduate and medical schools, and rabbinical seminary.

America has trained an increasing number of scholars who have gone on to teach Jewish studies in universities. Most leading universities of the country now have such courses in Judaica. Conservative

The Jewish Theological Seminary of America, in New York, housing library, schools and offices of all activities of the Conservative movement.

rabbis, as well as cantors and teachers, are graduated by the departments of the Seminary.

Hebrew Union College of Cincinnati, New York, and Los Angeles, combined with the Jewish Institute of Religion founded by Stephen S. Wise in New York, has added departments in music and education and has admitted women to its rabbinical school. Its rabbinical students are now required to study for one year in Israel.

Hebrew Union College in Cincinnati, which, combined with the Jewish Institute of Religion in New York, contains library and archives, schools and seminary of the Reform movement.

Besides building up these religious schools of higher learning, Jews have endowed Brandeis Univeristy, and have made contributions to many other secular colleges. In addition they support many community centers and a host of social service agencies, besides their synagogues and temples.

Jews Have Much to Be Concerned About

The Six Day War of 1967, in which the Israelis defeated the combined armies of many Arab states, worried Jews a great deal. There was much fear that the Arab leaders, backed by the large-scale military aid of the Soviet Union, might actually carry out their threat to push Israel into the sea—to destroy the people and their country. American Jews rallied to Israel's support as never before. They contributed tremendous sums of money and held meetings in every city. They gave heart to Israel's people, who snatched victory from what looked like sure defeat. But the Arabs still vow war, and the danger is still great.

Jews have been showing much concern, also, for Jews of the Soviet Union who wish to go to Israel, so they can live a Jewish life. American Jews have actively protested the difficulties the Russian government has placed in the way of living as Jews in the Soviet Union. They helped to keep the issue alive, and the Soviet Union has permitted many thousands to leave for Israel.

Jewish students in colleges across the nation have joined in many religious and cultural activities, and have published newspapers and magazines dealing with topics of Jewish interest. The name of this Philadelphia student paper, *Hayom*, means "Today".

American Jews are also worried about the quality of Jewish life in America. True, most Jewish families live in more comfortable homes than their immigrant ancestors did. They find it hard to believe that the kind of antisemitic discrimination grandparents talk about ever existed. They feel very much at home among neighbors who are very like themselves.

And it is true, also, that many Jewish children are today getting a better Jewish education than their parents did. Many go to summer camps that have Jewish study programs, and in which Hebrew is integrated into the camp activities. Others go on work-study tours to Israel during the summer, and some spend their junior year of college in study in Israel. But it is also true that many Jews, especially the youth, do not practice Judaism as the immigrants did in the

Demonstration in favor of Soviet Jewry and the desire of many to be free to emigrate to Israel. Young Jews in particular in America were inspired to support their struggle.

149

The ADL was founded in 1913 "to end the defamation of the Jewish people . . . and to secure justice and fair treatment for all people alike." It is one of the nation's oldest and leading Jewish human relations agencies.

early days. Fewer Jews go to services on Shabbat and holidays; the use of Yiddish has declined drastically; some homes have very little in them that is Jewish, and many parents do not send their children to Jewish schools at all. Many Jews are therefore concerned about the kind of Judaism there will be in the future.

This worry, however, is not shared by all Jews, for they see large numbers of young people interested in Jewish traditions and teachings, who enjoy their Jewish studies and seek meaningful Jewish experiences. There are substantial numbers who feel proud of their Jewish heritage. There are small groups of Jewish students on many college campuses who have joined together to seek a more intensive way of living as Jews. There are other groups that serve kosher meals and observe Shabbat together. Some are called *havurot* (or communes). And there are "Free Universities" that offer Jewish studies in some communities, courses in

such subjects as Hasidism, Hebrew, the novels of Elie Wiesel, or whatever the students, young and old, feel they want to learn. All this, of course, gives hope of a lively future for Judaism—different perhaps from the past, but creative and active in any case.

Jews live much like other Americans and share the problems of war, racism, pollution and poverty that all Americans face. There is a long tradition of social justice in Judaism, of trying to make life better for people. As human beings and as Jews, our people do their share to improve American life. Their interest in Israel and other Jewish matters does not stand in the way of their being Americans. The teachings of Judaism and the ideals of American democracy have many points in common. Young Jews of today, in carrying out the Jewish ideals of thirty-five centuries, can become better citizens of tomorrow, as Jews and as Americans, better even than their own parents.

Volunteers at Federation of Jewish Philanthropies of New York rally. The Federation raises millions of dollars for hospitals, Community Centers, schools, old age home, and Jewish education.

Dictionary

abolition: the idea that slavery in America should be ended

adhere: to stick to something

aliyah: going up, in Hebrew; usually means to settle in the land of Israel

ashkenazim: a Hebrew word that is often used when speaking of European Jews

astrolabe: an ancient instrument to measure the height of the stars

bereavement: a great loss, usually through death

bigotry: a refusal to accept any opinion or idea different from your own

broker: a person who acts as an agent for someone else buying or selling for him

burgher: word used for "citizen" some centuries ago

casualty: a person injured or killed in an accident or war

cheder: a room, in Hebrew; usually refers to one-room Hebrew elementary school

compulsory: something the law requires you to do, like attending elementary school

conscientious: one who gives himself completely to an idea or a cause

conversos: a Spanish word for one who changed his religion to become a Catholic

deeming: having a certain opinion about a person or idea

degenerate portion: part of the people who have lost some of the better qualities of the past

denomination: a religious group or movement

deportment: conduct or behavior of a person

discourse: a talk, lecture, or sermon

discrimination: being against a person on the basis of the group he belongs to, not because of personal record

Dissenters: English Protestants who refused to accept the Church of England

emancipation: freeing people from bondage to someone or something

ethnic: belonging to or coming from the racial, religious, or cultural customs of long ago

exemplary: something that can be praised, something good enough to be imitated

expedition: a journey or voyage for a specific purpose, like war or exploration

extremities: being in a condition of extreme need; suffering poverty

hazzan: a Hebrew word meaning a cantor; among Sephardim, he serves as the leader of the prayer service

immunities: special privileges, or exemptions from certain duties or services owed to a government

indigent: poor and needy, lacking food, clothing, etc.

Inquisition: a special group organized by the Catholic Church to find and punish those Catholics who practiced religious rituals that the Church did not teach or accept

invocation: an opening prayer at a public ceremony calling upon God for guidance

kashrut: a Hebrew word referring to the laws that make food religiously acceptable to an observant Jew

kibbutzim: a Hebrew word for Israeli agricultural communes in which all members work at assigned tasks and share equally in what is produced

kiddush: a Hebrew word for the blessing said over a cup of wine at the start of Shabbat or festivals

kipah: a Hebrew word for the little skull cap worn by Jews at a worship service

kosher: a Hebrew word that refers to the fitness of a food for an observant Jew to eat, or that the dishes are ritually clean, that is, that they are handled according to Jewish religious law

landsmanshaften: Yiddish word meaning organizations of Jews from the same section in Europe

leftist: a person who favors radical or great changes in a country's system of government or business

libel: to attack someone's good name or reputation falsely

lustre: radiance, merit, glory, a shining quality

mandate: the authority that was given to a nation to govern land that had belonged to Turkey or Germany, who had lost World War 1

mandated territory: land that had formerly been owned by Turkey or Germany, that was put in the hands of one of the countries that had won in World War 1—the land was not owned by the new country, but was to be governed for the League of Nations

Marranos: a Spanish word for Jews who had been converted to Christianity, but who were Jews at heart

151

matzot: the unleavened bread that Jews eat at Passover

medieval: referring to the style of life or thought of the Middle Ages of European history, especially the years from about 1000 to about 1500

mercenaries: people who work as soldiers, usually for a foreign power

Mikveh Israel: a Hebrew expression meaning "the gathering of the people Israel "

minhag: a Hebrew word meaning "custom" or procedure

minority rights: the rights of racial, religious or ethnic groups who are different from the majority group in a country—where there is *true democracy* all should have equal rights

minyan: a Hebrew word referring to the number who must be present for a public worship service, usually ten males

mitzvah: a Hebrew word meaning "commandment"—often refers to a "good deed "

mohel: a Hebrew word for the person who performs circumcisions

monastery: a place where persons who have taken religious vows live together as a group

monks: in Christianity, men who have joined a religious group and have taken vows to live together

Nordics: a type of human having tall stature, blond hair, blue eyes and a longish head; many such people have come from Scandinavia

open society: a system in which people of different racial, religious and ethnic backgrounds mingle together freely and equally

persecuted: people who are oppressed or injured or harmed because they believe in a religion or ideas that are unpopular

philanthropist: showing affection for mankind by giving money or property to people or organizations for the good of society

pogroms: a Russian word for organized attacks on people—in Russia it was most often against Jews

prediction: foretelling the future

prejudice: an unfavorable opinion about people formed even before knowing or understanding them

prophecy: it can mean making a prediction about what is to come in the future—or it can refer to a statement made by a divinely inspired religious person

quadrant: an instrument used in astronomy to measure altitudes

radical: a radical is one who believes the system should be thoroughly changed, even if it has to be done by force

refugees: people who have fled from their homes or countries to escape danger or great trouble

rehabilitated: restored to a condition of good health, or to a former rank or position

repugnant: distasteful, offensive, objectionable

sanction: support or approval for some action (no sanction would be no approval)

seceding: withdrawing from an alliance or federation; in the United States it referred to withdrawal from the Union by Southern States

seder: a Hebrew word for the special dinner on the first night of Passover; actually means "order."

seminary: a school for educating people for the rabbinate (or priesthood or ministry)

seraphim: angels or heavenly beings, often pictured as having a child's head surrounded by wings

Shabbat: a Hebrew word for the Jewish day of rest on Saturday, the seventh day of the week.

Shema: a Hebrew word meaning "Hear," the first word of a most important prayer (Hear, O Israel, the Lord our God, the Lord is One)

shohet: a Hebrew word for the person who slaughters animals for food according to rabbinic law

shtetl: a Yiddish word for the small towns in which Jews lived close to each other in European countries

shul: a Yiddish word for an orthodox synagogue

steerage: a part of a passenger ship where people traveled at the cheapest rate

talit: a Hebrew word for the shawl-like garment with fringes that is used during morning prayers

temporal: having to do with, or concerned with this world; in the Christian sense the word usually means something temporary

Tisha b'Av: Hebrew words meaning the ninth day of the month of Av; the name of a Jewish holiday

Tishri: the name of the seventh month in the Hebrew calendar

tzedakah: a Hebrew word meaning "righteous," which is usually translated as charity

universal air: the general air belonging to everyone, to all humanity

venerable: worthy of respect because of age, high office or dignified appearance

venerated: regarded with deep respect

yishuv: a Hebrew word for the Jewish community of Israel

INDEX